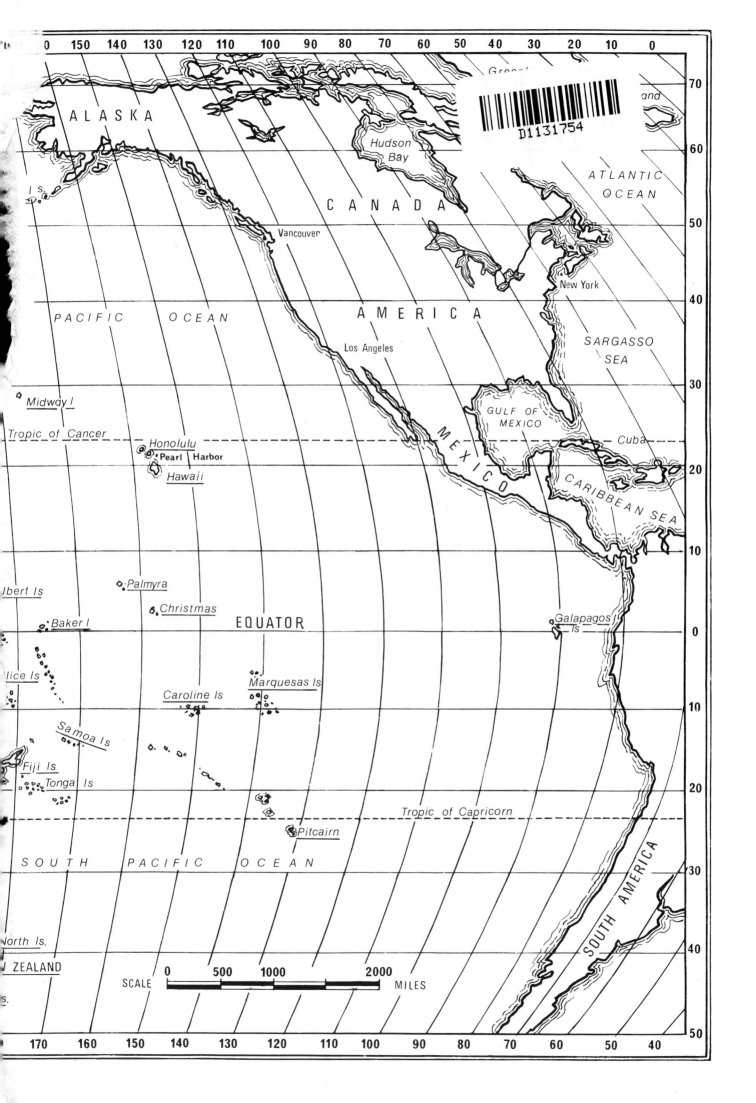

S. Borchardt

USAAF
at War in the
Pacific

USAAF
at War in the
Pacific

David Mondey and
Lewis Nalls

Charles Scribner's Sons
NEW YORK

Copyright © David Mondey & Lewis Nalls 1980

First U.S. edition published by Charles Scribner's Sons 1980

Copyright under the Berne Convention

All rights reserved. No part of this book
may be reproduced in any form without the
permission of Charles Scribner's Sons

1 3 5 7 9 11 13 15 17 19 I/C 20 18 16 14 12 10 8 6 4 2

Printed in Great Britain
Library of Congress Catalog Card Number 80-51368
ISBN 0-684-16702-6

Acknowledgements
To my ever-helpful friend, John W.R.
Taylor, for his knowledgeable advice; to
my equally good friend John Dennison who,
from the other side of the Atlantic, takes
time and trouble to make sure that my
historical facts are accurate; and especially to
Major General Otis C. Moore, USAF, for
his most generous Foreword.

Both Lewis Nalls and I would like also
to express our sincere appreciation to Virginia
C. Fincik of the USAF's Aerospace Audio-
Visual Service in Washington for her considerable help in locating specific photographs.
As for these photographs, which come from
United States Navy, Army and Air Force
archives, may we offer our thanks for
permission to reproduce them.

Dedicated to John Dennison, a historian of the United States Air Force, who gave generously of help and advice to a complete stranger. In the years since the first day of our meeting, friendship has made the Atlantic no wider than a narrow stream: may it always be so.

Contents

Title page: With the Marianas bases prepared the heavies began to fly in. A squadron of Liberators en route to Guam.

Left: This Thunderbolt arrived less conventionally, having mixed it with enemy flak en route.

Foreword

Perhaps it is a bit unusual for an American to write the foreword for a book written by an English author. However, the book concerns itself with the United States Air Force and that, I believe, establishes my prerogative.

Mr Mondey compiles the large section about United States aircraft in *Jane's All the World's Aircraft* and had previously prepared *A Pictorial History of the USAF*; hence he must be considered an authority on the subject.

Even before my tour as Chief of Staff, Seventh Air Force, South Vietnam, I was interested in what US historians had to say about World War II in the Pacific, as well as what historians from other countries emphasised – and, more particularly, how the events of World War II and its postwar period had an impact upon the future conflict in Southeast Asia. We must study history to refrain from false steps gained through the uncertainty of the unknown or the trauma which comes from repeating mistakes once already experienced.

I am confident from my experience in the Orient that the area will be influencing our history for years to come. For that reason, I submit Mr Mondey's book as a part of that Oriental and Pacific history with which men ought to acquaint themselves.

Major-General Otis C. Moore, USAF (Retd)

Right: B-24 Liberators leave behind a pall of smoke as they provide pre-invasion air strikes.

Introduction

Within the scope of this book it is impossible to cover in detail the contribution made by the United States Army Air Force (USAAF) to victory against Japan in World War II. In fact, in many instances, it is difficult to study in isolation the work of the USAAF, because it was so closely integrated with that of the US Navy, US Marine Corps and the Royal Australian Air Force (RAAF). Thus, a broad outline, leading from the first devastating shock at Pearl Harbor to the surrender table aboard the USS *Missouri*, must needs pick out only the most significant actions.

Details of the Doolittle Raid on Tokyo, and of the Battles of the Coral Sea and Midway, are given briefly and somewhat out of context in Chapter VI, since they have already been covered in more detail in my earlier *Pictorial History of the USAF*.

In the above-mentioned book, Lewis Nalls of Alexandria, Virginia, a highly-experienced American photo-researcher, helped me by finding most of the illustrations. For this book we have joined forces and he has been solely responsible for the superb selection of photographs which, by themselves, provide excellent coverage of the bitterly-fought actions in the Pacific theatre.

The first chapter will, I hope, set the scene and answer the question as to why the Japanese became involved in what most military planners would have considered a hopeless task. And to comment on their opening gambit I feel compelled to borrow 11 extremely suitable words attributed to the Old Testament prophet Hosea:

> *They have sown the wind, and they*
> *shall reap the whirlwind.*

Surbiton, 1979 *DM and LN*

Right: Slowly but surely strength began to build up to blaze the long trail back. Here B-25s of the 42nd Bomb Group at Stirling Island in the Solomons prepare for take-off to New Guinea.

1
The Day of Infamy

Right: To the cheers of their comrades, the first of the attackers leaves the carrier deck of one of Vice-Adm Nagumo's task force at dawn on 7 December 1941. Target: Pearl Harbor.

Against the piles of the jetty the water rose and fell sluggishly to the swell of the Pacific, its surface blanketed by a scum of oil that inhibited movement: in its viscous mass floated the rubbish of life and death. Here and there sunlight glinted in an irridescent rainbow on a thinner patch of oil, perhaps the only hint of brightness in a sombre scene. A stench of burned material filled the air: burnt wood, burnt paint, burnt flesh. But it was the fumes of oil and petrol that dominated all else, for clouds of thick oily smoke still sought to eclipse the sun, and every available petrol-driven pump phut-phutted away in the hopeless task of salvaging the remnants of the US Pacific Fleet. Along the length of Battleship Row Pearl Harbor, weary men in filthy uniforms dejectedly ministered to the crippled pride of the US Navy which, within a few minutes of time, had been damaged severely, was sinking or had been sunk.

How had such an event come to pass: one which President Roosevelt announced to a joint session of Congress with the words: 'Yesterday, 7 December 1941 -- a date which will live in infamy -- the United States of America was suddenly and deliberately attacked by naval and air forces of the Empire of Japan.'

To find the whole answer it would be necessary to turn back the calendar many years, but for our purpose it will suffice to recall that in 1931 Japan abandoned her

policy of conciliation towards China and, on a trumped-up pretext, began military operations in Manchuria. Despite intervention by the League of Nations, at the end of 1931 Japan had overrun some 200,000sq miles (518,000sq km) of Manchuria and, in early 1932, a large Japanese force was landed at Shanghai. As the 1930s advanced, operations against China continued in a policy of land expansion.

Little was done, or could be done, by the League of Nations to end or limit this conflict. Japan could feel fairly satisfied with progress on land. At sea it was a different matter. The Washington Naval Treaty of 1921 and the London Naval Conference of 1930 had, by mutual discussion and agreement, limited the naval powers of the United States, Great Britain, Japan, France and Italy, although the two latter countries failed to ratify their agreements after the London meeting. When, in 1936, new proposals were made to limit the aircraft carrier fleets of the same nations, Japan walked out.

Just over 12 months after the outbreak of World War II, on 27 September 1940, Germany, Italy and Japan signed a mutual assistance pact in Berlin. Inspired by Hitler, it aimed at limiting the scope of the European war by hinting at a new and determined partnership that would 'frighten off' the United States, and might prevent active or indirect intervention in the European theatre.

Below: This Japanese photograph shows the first signs of attack on Pearl Harbor, but Battleship Row is still unscathed.

Right: A direct hit on the USS *Shaw* was soon to bring a change to the Navy's disciplined lines.

Below right: Only minutes later Pearl Harbor presented a scene of unforgettable disaster.

Its only immediate effect was to Japan's disadvantage, for it encouraged Britain to reopen the Burma Road in October, providing a new munitions life-line to China's defenders.

The collapse of France and Holland in 1940 led to extremist demands from Japan, who insisted that supplies for China through French Indo-China to Chungking, and through Burma and Hong Kong must cease. When they continued to reach the Chinese, Japan occupied Indo-China. But in reality this was a far deeper ploy, representing the first move towards securing vast new territories for the Japanese Co-Prosperity Sphere, a plan under which Japanese militarists saw their country the master of the Orient.

Neither America nor Britain could allow such a move to go unchallenged and both governments applied economic sanctions. Before there could be any useful discussion to resolve Japanese-American problems, the United States insisted that Japan must:

1 Cease aggression in China and withdraw her forces.
2 Sever her ties with the Axis powers.
3 Terminate her penetration of Indo-China, undertaking to make no further expansion to the south or south-west.

This, for Japan, was the last straw. Paramount was the fact that she depended upon America for many strategic materials, the most vital

of which was aviation fuel. In mid-1941 she had reasonable stocks, but without continuing supplies from America the demands of the war against China would liquidate those within 12 months. Her only other sources of supply were Indonesia and South America. Japanese-Dutch negotiations for Indonesian supplies were ended by instigation of the Allies; and the United States slammed the South American door.

The militarist group of the Japanese Army, who had boiled up the invasion of Manchuria in 1931, had become all powerful in Japan. Despite opposition by the Navy and non-military members of the government, they insisted that the country's only hope of salvation lay in war. If they waited for endless diplomatic negotiations, they argued, fuel stocks would become exhausted and the Chinese – whose resistance had stiffened with the renewal of supplies – might throw them out of the hard-won territories. The only solution was war against the West, without delay, with the prime aim of seizing the Indonesian oilfields.

The Japanese Navy was opposed to such action, as careful study had convinced its planners that the country could not survive a long war. Naval strength would allow initial success, but the strategists were convinced that unless the enemy could be virtually eliminated within a very short period of time, the vast productive potential of the Americans and her Allies would prove overwhelming.

There was, however, one man in the Japanese Navy who, almost 12 months earlier, had already considered how to strike the Americans such a devastating blow that Japan might seize all the bases she needed before the United States and her Allies could react. This was not the brainstorm of a fanatic, but the carefully studied plan of a man who knew the Western world: a man who might almost be described as the Billy Mitchell of Japanese military aviation, for it is recorded that in 1915 he had commented to a newspaper reporter: '... the most important warship of the future will be one that carries aeroplanes.'

This was Isoroku Yamamoto, a vital contributor to the establishment of a powerful navy air force. Study in America and his deep appreciation of naval strategy brought selection as leader of the Japanese delegation to the London Naval Conference. When, subsequently, Japan advised America and Britain that she no longer considered herself bound by the treaty, it was Yamamoto who argued constantly with navy planners to establish the vital importance of aircraft carriers to island Japan.

His years of study in America had enabled Yamamoto to appreciate the production potential and material resources of that vast country, and he was one of the first to realise that the Army's ignorance of these factors could prove disastrous to his country if conventional military tactics were followed. So strong were his fears on this point that he was impelled to write to a close friend: '.... Should hostilities break out between Japan and the United States, it is not enough that we take Guam and the Philippines, nor

Left: In dry dock, the destroyers USS *Cassin* and *Downes* lie shattered: behind them is the mighty bulk of the flagship, USS *Pennsylvania*.

Below: The destruction of the USS *Arizona* marked the end of an era for naval planners who, for so long, had argued the invincibility of a battleship when confronted by the upstart aeroplane.

even Hawaii and San Francisco. We would have to march into Washington and sign the treaty in the White House. I wonder if our politicians (who speak so lightly of a Japanese-American war) have confidence as to the outcome and are prepared to make the necessary sacrifices.'

Admiral I. Yamamoto, Commander-in-Chief of the Japanese Fleet, spared neither himself nor his men to perfect the art of aircraft/ship warfare. By the time of the Fleet's manoeuvres in the spring of 1940, he had brought the entire naval team to a peak of efficiency. And it was at about this same time that he first began to consider how a surprise attack on Pearl Harbor might achieve such a devastating blow against the American Pacific Fleet that Japan's Navy would gain freedom of movement throughout the Pacific, allowing the seizure of territories to deprive the West of bases in the Far East. Furthermore, each territorial conquest would provide either new living space for the homeland's teaming millions, or vital raw materials that would strengthen her economy and independence.

The idea became a proposal, passed to naval planners. By April 1941 Operation Z, as it became designated, had come up against only one major snag: how to ensure that the aerial torpedoes carried by the Navy's aircraft could be launched successfully in the shallow waters of Pearl Harbor. While the Fleet's aircraft practised daily and endlessly in simulated attacks against a long jetty in Kagoshima harbour, torpedo specialists worked around the clock to perfect a weapon that could be launched in shallow waters.

All through the long summer the training continued, and as autumn approached Yamamoto took his plan to Tokyo for evaluation and approval by the Navy's General Staff. The discussions went on and on: the staff were not enthusiastic. Primary concern was the fear that two or three of their precious aircraft carriers might be lost. None believed that the US Pacific Fleet could be destroyed, for like traditional navy men around the world they had no appreciation that the still frail aeroplane could eliminate the armoured might of a battleship. Yamamoto's arguments were useless: Admiral Ngano, Chief of the General Staff, would not authorise the plan.

A lesser man would have given up there and then. Not so Yamamoto, who closed his mind to what he considered just plain old-fashioned thinking and went ahead with training. Then, at a suitable moment, he proffered his resignation. The threat proved adequate: authority was given for Operation Z to proceed.

In early November 1941 Yamamoto ordered the task force to put to sea, ship by ship spread over some days, so that to any interested observers their sailings would appear unrelated. The heavy carriers *Akagi, Kaga, Shokaku* and *Zuikaku,* the lighter class *Hiryu* and *Soryu,* accompanied by two battleships, three cruisers, nine destroyers, three submarines and eight oil tankers, moved individually to their rendezvous point. In the void they had left, within Japan's inland sea area, normal ship-to-ship and ship-to-shore wireless traffic was maintained spuriously to fox enemy monitors of the true position of the Fleet.

After a final conference in the *Akagi,* on 26 November, the combined fleet put its nose into the icy seas of a foggy dawn, sailing towards the Hawaiian Islands. On 2 December Admiral Nagumo received from Yamamoto the coded signal: 'Climb Mount Niitaka'. Please note the date, for at that moment the task force was committed to the planned attack.

In America there was certainly no national concern at that moment regarding the situation in the Pacific. The news from Europe was increasingly bad, but since it was most unlikely that Germany would strike at the United States there was little need to fear involvement. Far more worrying was the question of the effect that Roosevelt's new (March 1941) Lend-Lease Act might have on individual taxation, for non-participation in the war that had been raging in Europe and the Middle East for over two years had brought new prosperity.

It would have needed a very discerning person to appreciate the implications of a tiny news paragraph which appeared in some national newspapers on 12 October 1941. It reported only that three passenger liners were being despatched from Tokyo to evacuate Japanese nationals from the United States.

Above: No less destructive was the attack on USAAF bases. Installations were soon burning on Hickham Field.

Above right: No matter where you looked destruction was, by Japanese standards, superb. Wrecked aircraft litter the apron at Wheeler Field.

Centre right: Yamamoto had trained his Navy flyers well, their bombing accuracy was of the highest order. No 3 Hangar, Wheeler Field.

Below right: Rear view of No 11 Hangar, Hickham Field.

Behind the scenes in America, however, there were no illusions regarding the gravity of the situation. While the game of diplomacy was being played in Washington, where the Japanese ambassadors Kurusu and Nomura were maintaining a front of cordial negotiation, the War Department was busy doing its utmost to strengthen the defences of the south-west Pacific and the Philippine Islands, a highly sensitive area in the war plans of the Allied powers. America hoped that the combined potential of its Pacific Fleet at Oahu and the rapid establishment of powerful land and air forces in the Philippines would prove sufficient to make Japan adopt a cautious policy.

In retrospect, it seems strange that the Japanese were able so easily to overwhelm the defences at Pearl Harbor. Way back in 1935 Billy Mitchell had predicted: '. . . Hawaii is swarming with Japanese spies. As I have said before, that's where the blow will be struck – on a fine, quiet Sunday morning.' There had been other straws in the wind. Early in 1941 a Japanese diplomat had indiscreetly leaked the information that the American Pacific Fleet might suddenly and mysteriously be eliminated. US Ambassador Joseph C. Grew had this information in January and advised the US Government, who in turn passed the tit-bit of news to Admiral Husband E. Kimmel, the naval commander at Pearl Harbor. Any faith that Kimmel might have placed on that information must have been destroyed by a covering note from US naval intelligence, which commented that they disbelieved such a blatant rumour.

Even as late as 27 November, General Marshall advised General MacArthur that negotiations with the Japanese had reached a virtual stalemate and to be prepared for any eventuality. One point was emphatic, how-

17

ever: Japan, not America, must be the first aggressor. Finally, on 4 December in Japan General Hideki Tojo, Japanese Premier and Minister of War, demanded boldly that American and British exploitation of the Asiatic peoples should end. World radio reported his words, including the final comment that '. . . . . their exploitation would be purged and avenged.'

America's problems in respect of Pacific defence were manifold. Paramount were the immense distances involved, for the Pacific Ocean occupies almost half of the Earth's surface, stretching 9,455 miles (15,215km) from the Bering Straits to the Antarctic and is, at its broadest, 10,492 miles (16,885km) across. A Pan American Sikorsky S-42, the *China Clipper*, had made a pioneering crossing from San Francisco to Manila, via Hawaii, Midway, Wake and Guam Islands, but it was not until 22 November 1935, that a Martin M130 flying-boat of the same name made the first route-proving flight carrying mail and light freight: thereafter the Martin 'boats maintained a once-a-week service until the advent of the Boeing 314 Clipper. Long range with worthwhile payload was still a rare combination, and hence the desperate need for America to ensure the security of her vital stepping stones across the Pacific.

It was clear that despite naval domination of the Pacific defence role until that time, the moment had arrived when the United States Army Air Force (USAAF) must play a part in this theatre. How well was it prepared for the task?

The conventional Navy versus Air Force controversy had ended in virtual stalemate after the death of Billy Mitchell, the one American most convinced that the aeroplane was the battleship's master. His gospel had continued to echo around the corridors of Army and Navy headquarters for some time after his death, but naval planners remained adamant that the aeroplane posed no serious problems for their latest, greatest and most advanced battleships. If any news of the British Fleet Air Arm's success against the Italian Fleet in Taranto Harbour on 11 November 1941, or of the sinking of the *Bismarck* on 27 May 1941, had reached their ears, they gave no indications. It did not end with the aeroplane versus battleship argument.

From early aviation days the Navy had maintained stubbornly that airpower was incapable of defending America's vast coastlines. Only the tried and proven arm of

Top: Practically nothing had escaped. The interior of No 1 Hangar, Wheeler Field.

Above: Even in the dispersal areas there was nothing but shattered wrecks of aircraft.

sea power was adequate for such a vital task. Time had done nothing to change their attitude. The long-range bomber and reconnaissance aircraft for which the USAAC had fought for over many years were virtually blocked by naval power in the administration. Only penny-packet numbers of strategic bombers evolved. Even the USAAC's Army parent still believed that the aeroplane's only effective role was in support of troops on the ground, and this meant that the air arm was equipped predominantly with aircraft consonant with this belief.

Thus, in mid-1941, there were only a handful of Boeing B-17 Flying Fortresses: even they were considered extravagant by the Navy and useless by the Army. Few planners of any nation had taken heed of the shrewd comment made by France's Marshal Foch soon after World War I: '... military minds always believe that the next war will be ... the same ... as the last. That has never been the case and never will be ...'

The manpower situation was little better. Lt-Gen Lewis H. Brereton has recorded that on 1 October 1941, USAAF's Combat Command could muster only 530 pilots qualified for combat operations, comprising:

	Heavy Bombers	Medium Bombers	Light Bombers	Fighters
1st pilots	90	72	25	171
2nd pilots	64	108	—	—

It was against such a background of unpreparedness that Lewis Brereton, then a major-general, was despatched to the Pacific theatre on 21 October 1941, to assume command of the Far East Air Force (FEAF), which was desperately short of aircraft, pilots, ground crews and the most mundane requirements of an operational air force. He had been selected for this task as his long experience of logistics and maintenance would be valuable in expanding this force as rapidly as circumstances would permit.

His first stop, at Oahu, showed that unpreparedness was not limited to the homeland. This outpost lacked even rudimentary warning of impending air attack. Midway had two good concrete runways and little else. Wake was defended by a firm opinion that they would be the first target of the Japanese. The garrison of Guam had

Below: On 8 December 1941, President Roosevelt tells a packed House of Congress of the 'day of infamy'.

practically no defences, and because of their close proximity to a strongly held Japanese island already suffered psychological defeat by being firmly convinced that they would be completely eliminated by the first enemy attack.

At Manila, Brereton met General Douglas MacArthur, who believed there was little likelihood of any Japanese aggression before the spring of 1942. Inspection of the HQ of the FEAF revealed the same pitiful tale: it comprised a ridiculously small establishment steeped in peacetime island traditions. The most unlikely thing that could happen to them was to become involved in anyone's war.

Brereton discovered there were then only two airfields from which B-17s could operate: Clark Field which had good facilities and Del Monte, on Mindano Island, which had good runways but no other facilities. A third airfield, Nichols Field adjacent to Manila, was in process of having its runways lengthened and a new one constructed. Total combat aircraft strength then amounted to 35 B-17s, a few Douglas B-18 medium bombers, 28 Seversky P-35s and 72 Curtiss P-40 Warhawk fighters. In addition, the Philippines Air Force had 12 Boeing P-26 fighters. There were virtually no spares and equipment, and only the most elementary tools available for maintenance.

At all his stopping places Brereton had issued a string of orders to start things moving, to bring in men, supplies, equipment, weapons and aircraft. With the initial moves made, MacArthur despatched Brereton to Australia to arrange the preparation of air bases in the northern territories. There, with the fullest co-operation of Air Chief Marshal Sir Charles Burnett, RAAF, an American ferry route was planned across Australia, as was the establishment of airfields and training bases. On 26 November, the day that Brereton began his return journey to Manila, the Japanese task force set sail from its rendezvous point.

Following the receipt of Yamamoto's coded signal that the attack on Pearl Harbor was to

Left: Engine changing, especially in the open air, always seems a most untidy business. This P-39 at Townsville, Australia, looks something of a wreck.

Below: A few days later, nicely polished for maximum speed, it once again looks like an aeroplane.

Above left: Immediately after Pearl Harbor there was little in the way of aircraft to strike back at the enemy. Maid of all work for long-range tasks was the Boeing B-17 Fortress.

Left: Typical of the fighter opposition was the Boeing P-26 that had equipped the Philippines Air Force, armed with only two forward-firing machine guns.

Below left: The faster four-gun Seversky P-35s of the USAAF had been reduced from 48 to eight in the first two days of the war. It proved to be the operational debut and finale of the type.

Bottom left: Most valuable of the early fighters was the Bell P-39 Airacobra with its unconventional mid-fuselage mounted engine. This was to allow installation of a 37mm cannon in the nose which, together with six machine guns, made it a hard-hitting machine. They were pushed out to Australia, Hawaii and New Guinea as fast as circumstances would allow.

be launched, activity on the Japanese carriers rose to a peak as crews were briefed meticulously for the impending operation. Mechanics did their best to ensure, over and over again, that no aircraft would let down its country or pilot; armourers checked and re-checked the guns and bomb releases that would take war to the despised Americans.

On 6 December the historic 'Z' flag, which Admiral Heihachiro Togo had flown when Japan had won the great naval victory at Tsushima in 1905, was raised to *Akagi*'s masthead. Standing to attention as well as the plunging carrier deck would allow, pilots and their crews heard the final rallying message from their commander-in-chief: '... The moment has arrived. The rise or fall of our Empire is at stake ...' As their cheers were torn to silent shreds by the freshening wind, the flag almost hidden from view in lowering skies, the fleet turned south to Oahu, now 400 miles (644km) distant.

At dawn on 7 December 1941, Nagumo's task force had reached its fly-off point, some 275 miles (443km) north of Pearl Harbor. In two waves a total of 245 dive and torpedo bombers, escorted by 108 Zero fighters, struck at the US Fleet, and pounded Hickham

Field, Wheeler Field and Ford Island, as well as a seaplane base at Kaneoke Bay. In minutes they had devastated the American Fleet, and claimed to have destroyed 104 fighter and 37 bomber aircraft on the ground. The Americans put their own losses as 188 aircraft, 18 ships sunk or seriously damaged, over 2,000 men killed and around 2,000 more injured. The cost to the Japanese had been just 29 aircraft, comprising five torpedo and fifteen dive bombers, plus nine Zero fighters.

Long before the first aircraft landed Nagumo had learned from the flight commander, Mitsuo Fuchida, of the overwhelming success of the attack. The news came in due course to the battleship *Yamoto*, at anchor in the harbour of Hiroshima, where Admiral Yamamoto and his staff waited anxiously for reports of the action. Their elation at success was tempered on the following day when American radio broadcasts left little doubt that national public opinion was united as never before and that the nation was seething for revenge. Only time would reveal the true victor.

And it is strange, is it not, that Hiroshima was significantly involved both in the beginning and the end.

2
Expansion, and the First Contraction

Left: The Curtiss P-40 Warhawk, seen here, and the Bell P-39, were to represent the main front-line fighter types of the USAAF for some 18 months from April 1942.

Almost simultaneously with their attack on Pearl Harbor, the Japanese had landed invading forces in Malaya and made their first air strikes against the Philippines and Hong Kong. Two days later they made initial landings on the northern coast of Luzon, quickly seizing the airfields at Aparri and Vigan so that their aircraft could harry the remnants of the FEAF.

Britain had despatched the battleships *Prince of Wales* and *Repulse* to Singapore, which they had reached on 2 December. With news of Japanese landings at Koto Bharu and Singora on 8 December, the British Admiral Tom Phillips deemed it essential to strike at the enemy without delay. Two days later, without air cover, both warships were sunk by Japanese aircraft. Thus, within the short space of three days, there were no American or British capital ships available for operations within the Indian or Pacific Oceans. Air power had given the Japanese mastery of these vast sea areas.

They were not slow to take full advantage of the situation, for not only were they relieved of the threat of any major naval action, but it was also clear that there was little danger likely to come from the skies. By early 1942 the Japanese had swept through Siam to Burma, had captured Penang, Hong Kong and the greater part of the British Malay peninsula and were strengthening their hold on the Philippines.

It was here that American and Filipino troops under General Douglas MacArthur staged a heroic resistance, aided by an air force which on 11 December had been reduced to 16 B-17s, 28 P-40s and five P-35s. Fighting for every inch of land and every vital minute of time, they succeeded in holding out until 7 May 1942, when MacArthur's commander in the field, Maj-Gen J.M. 'Skinny' Wainwright, was forced to surrender.

But before that moment came, the pitifully small representative force of the USAAF had gained some success despite appalling odds. To add to the problems, pro-Japanese Filipinos pin-pointed aircraft and installations by signal fires or flares to guide attacking aircraft. Food and sleep were minimal, cleanliness non-existent, and the lack of tools and equipment made every sortie a saga of courage.

Among those who triumphed over the endless difficulties was Lt 'Buzz' Wagner of the 17th Pursuit Squadron, soon awarded a Distinguished Service Cross for fearless attacks against Japanese aircraft operating from Vigan. Within a mere 10 days he had gained five victories in the air, and his score was increased by many aircraft destroyed on the ground.

But courage alone could not defeat the steadily increasing numbers of Japanese. The inevitable moment came when the tiny remaining force was too precious to risk in combat. On Christmas Eve 1941, Brereton was ordered to transfer HQ FEAF to northern Australia, which he reached just before the end of the month.

The first three months of the year were a disastrous period, for without adequate air support the Allies were helpless to stop Japanese progress. Hong Kong, Malaya, the Philippines, Netherlands East Indies, Burma, and the Andamans and most of Borneo was in enemy hands; and when the Japanese cut the Burma Road, supplies to China came to a halt.

The first check on Japanese expansion came in early April when an attempt to land on Ceylon was frustrated by Fulmar and Hurricane aircraft based on that island.* The Battle of the Coral Sea in May, during which the Japanese light carrier *Shoho* was sunk and the *Shokaku* severely damaged, brought to an end a first attempt to capture Port Moresby, New Guinea. But the most serious blow to Japan's naval power came in June, off Midway, when the carriers *Akagi, Hiryu, Kaga* and *Soryu* were sunk by torpedo-bombers of the US carriers *Enterprise, Hornet* and *Yorktown*. It was a major victory for American air power; the turning point of the war in the Pacific; and the end of the road for naval planners of all nations who might still believe that naval power was impregnable to attack from the air.

*Described by John W. R. Taylor in *Pictorial History of the RAF*, Volume II (Ian Allan).

Above: So desperate was the need for fighters that anything that could stagger into the air was invaluable. *Spare Parts*, illustrated, was a sort of Heinz P-39, with bits of P-40s and other lesser types, built by the group of men in the photograph.

Above right: One of the most valuable new arrivals was the Consolidated B-24 Liberator, needed to supplement the B-17s, for most worthwhile missions were long-range. The local Gooney birds soon accepted them as natural fauna . . .

Centre right: . . . and even found that a bomb dump could be adopted as a convenient nesting place.

Below right: Improvisation was the keynote of the early days. Gen Kenney's parafragmentation bombs for low-level deployment were typical, seen here straddling an enemy machine.

By this time the FEAF had ceased to exist, its remnants of units in Australia being grouped together as the nucleus of the 5th Air Force under the overall command of Maj-Gen George C. Kenney. Together with the Royal Australian Air Force (RAAF), they were quickly faced with serious problems as the Japanese threatened New Guinea. If the latter could become established there in strength, their bomber aircraft would be able to menace northern Australia.

Early in 1942 Japanese forces seized New Britain and the bulk of the Solomon Islands. From New Britain their bombers began to blast Lae and Salamaua on New Guinea, and when invading forces followed in strength it was clear that the enemy were intent on controlling the entire island, including the important Allied base at Port Moresby, only some 170 miles (274km) distant from Salamaua. It was fortunate that the Owen Stanley range of mountains intervened, for there was then little else to stop the invaders from overrunning Moresby.

Events took a far more serious turn on 21 July 1942, when the enemy began new landings at Buna, little more than 100 miles (161km) from Moresby, and from where a road led to a pass through the mountains, beyond Kokada. Limited strikes by the 5th Air Force B-17s and Martin B-26 Marauders represented the only opposition that could be offered, and even these had very limited success. As darkness came, new landings were made at Gona.

With some 4,000-5,000 troops ashore, the Japanese began a crossing of the Owen Stanley range, and hastily-mustered Australian units were pushed back steadily towards

Left: Another urgent need was aircrew training. With no aircraft or fuel to spare for air-to-air practice, gunners had to learn the theory from ground mock-ups.

Below: Eventually came the exciting and rare moment to let off a few shells against an airborne towed target.

Bottom: When it came to operations the gunners had a hard life. Hours of concentrated boredom, brief moments of heart-thumping action, and usually with destruction of their own aircraft the penalty for failure.

Moresby, where enemy bombers were busy softening up defences and airfields.

The defenders possessed fighters, Bell P-39 Airacobras, P-400s (the designation applied to P-39s that had been under construction for the British, and were re-possessed after Pearl Harbor) and Curtiss P-40 Warhawks. Unfortunately, the early versions of these aircraft had inadequate rate of climb, and there was no high-pressure oxygen for the pilots available in New Guinea: the enemy soon discovered that by coming in at altitudes above 22,000ft (6,700m) they were virtually unmolested.

But if the Airacobras were impotent at altitude, it was a very different story at sea level. When the 35th Fighter Group's machines were used as close-support ground strafers for the 'Diggers', the combination proved good enough to stop the Japanese from entering Moresby.

The 5th Air Force should also have been able to deploy two light bomber types at this period, the Douglas A-20 and A-24, but the A-20s had inadequate fire power as delivered and were being modified in Australia by the addition of four nose-mounted 0.5in machine guns, and their desperately short range increased by the addition of two 450gal (1,703 litre) bomb bay tanks. No suitable bombs were available for use in a low-level close-support role, so on Gen Kenney's suggestion, 23lb fragmentation bombs with small parachutes attached to delay their fall were adopted, and each machine could carry 40 or more of these weapons.

The A-24, an Air Force version of the Navy's SBD dive bomber, poorly armed, slow, and with inadequate fuel capacity, was found to be so vulnerable that it was relegated to non-combat missions.

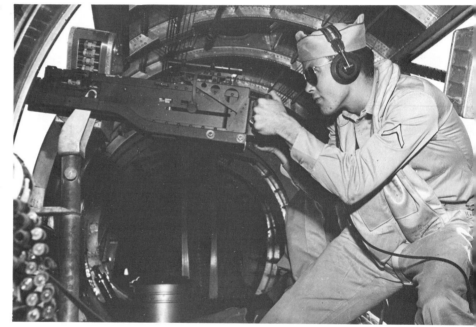

With the enemy advance on Moresby brought to a halt, the next step was to eject him from the beachhead at Buna. This was not in line with Japanese plans, who began to reinforce their base there during September and October. Under cover of darkness fresh troops and supplies were brought in by small coastal vessels from Lae and Salamaua.

Despite this, the Australians kept pushing slowly ahead, their supply line maintained by native carriers and air drop, while every available machine was employed to blast the Japanese supply lines and their base camp at Buna.

The first essential was air strips into which transports could operate. At Wanigela, some 65 miles (105km) south-west of Buna, aircraft dropped a small number of Australian officers who, in collaboration with native labourers, began to burn off the kanui grass. Soon Australian engineers were flown in, and with machetes, cane knives and sheer guts they hacked out an airstrip. By 17 October a strip had been prepared at Sapia, and from there the American engineers prepared a series of strips as they moved down to the coast at Dyke Ackland Bay. There, only 23 miles (37km) from Buna, they had a strip available for operation by 4 November. Of more importance was the strip established at Dobodura, only 15 miles (24km) from Buna, for it was in a situation that seemed ideal for construction of a large base for future operations. By 21 November its first strip was operational; three weeks later engineers had built three more, one of 4,200ft (1,280m) in length.

As soon as the strips were ready air transport began the task of hauling in men and equipment. Some measure of this effort is given by the fact that between 13 November and 23 January 1943, more than 2,000 tons of supplies were flown in. On 26 November three Douglas DC-3s delivered to Dobodura a 105mm howitzer, its tractor, guncrew and an initial 100 rounds of ammunition.

As the infantry began their attacks on Buna they received close support from the specially converted A-20s, which showered the enemy with the para-fragmentation bombs, while North American B-25 Mitchells of the 345th Bombardment Group dropped more conventional bombs from 6,000ft (1,830m). It was anticipated that Buna would fall on the following day, 20 November, but the Allies had not counted on the tenacity of the enemy who had taken every possible advantage of the low-lying, swampy terrain. Heavy logs reinforced with sheet metal, ammunition boxes packed with sand, rocks, steel drums and even coconuts, provided the fortifications which they defended with fanatical courage.

By the end of November the Allied advance had bogged down: for the first time came an understanding of what it was going to cost in men and materials to dislodge the Japanese from the island stepping-stones that lead to their homeland.

It is for this reason that we examine the Papuan campaign in some detail. Extracts from a letter sent by General Kenney to General Arnold provide a frame for the overall picture as seen then by the Commander of the 5th Air Force:

'Tanks and heavy artillery can be reserved for the battlefields of Europe and Africa. They have no place in jungle warfare. The artillery in this theatre flies, the light mortar and machine guns, the rifle, tommygun, grenade and knife are the weapons carried by men who fly to war, jump in parachutes, are carried in gliders and who land from air transports on ground which air engineers have prepared . . .

Below: Neither was there any sophisticated interpretation of the all-too-few reconnaissance photographs. You just did your best with simple tools.

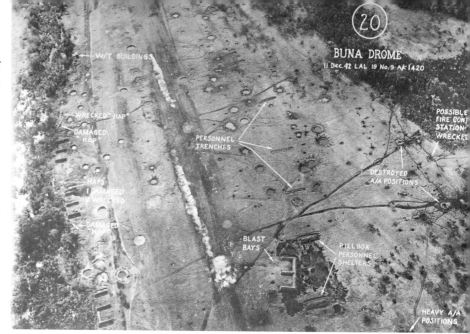

BUNA DROME
11 Dec. 42 LAL 19 No.9 AK1420

W/T BUILDINGS

WRECKED "HAP"

DAMAGED HAP

HAPS DAMAGED & WRECKED

DAMAGED HAP

PERSONNEL TRENCHES

BLAST BAYS

PILLBOX PERSONNEL SHELTERS

POSSIBLE FIRE CONT STATION WRECKED

DESTROYED A/A POSITIONS

HEAVY A/A POSITIONS

'In the Pacific theatre we have a number of islands garrisoned by small forces. These islands are nothing more or less than aerodromes or aerodrome areas from which modern fire-power is launched. Sometimes they are true islands like Wake or Midway, sometimes they are localities on large land masses. Port Moresby, Lae and Buna are all on the island of New Guinea, but the only practicable way to get from one to the other is by air or by water: they are all islands as far as warfare is concerned. Each is garrisoned by a small force and each can be taken by a small force once local air control is secured. Every time one of these islands is taken, the rear is better secured . . .'

The task ahead was clear: to capture these 'islands', secure the rear, and move steadily nearer to the Japanese homeland. But it was essential to provide the troops on the ground with more effective close-support: in addition to the A-20s and B-25s, there were also some Martin B-26 Marauders and a squadron of RAAF Beaufighters. A far greater problem than the paucity of aircraft, however, was the question of communication. Liaison was based initially on advance requests for air support, and was therefore useless in fluid situations. How could a platoon commander make an overnight request for support in an attack against a target of whose existence he was then unaware? When faced with the need for air support – which he couldn't get until tomorrow – should he wait for 24 hours? To make matters worse, targets of vital importance, such as strongpoints, were frequently hidden by a featureless sea of jungle through which an airman had virtually no chance of finding and hitting his target.

It was a moment when the World War I technique of artillery combined with aerial spotting was needed, and the latter was

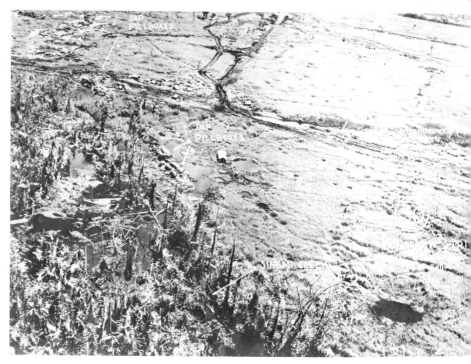

JAP PILLBOXES

JAP PILLBOXES

SINEMI CREEK

Top: Some of the coverage provided by improvisations was pretty good by any standards. This and the photograph above show that Buna airfield and the adjacent airstrip and defences were well documented before the beginning of attacks to throw the Japanese out.

Left: Despite the distances and lack of reconnaissance aircraft, every attempt was made to keep a close watch on the enemy. Japanese-held Wake Island in early 1941.

provided mainly by RAAF Wirraways. Slow and vulnerable, but flown courageously by their pilots, they proved effective but suffered serious losses.

By early January the elimination of Buna as an enemy base was nearing its end. The bitter hand-to-hand fighting that was needed to mop up the area lasted until 23 January and, in the closing stages, the troops had little need of direct air support. It was as well, for the 5th Air Force required all its strength in men and machines to fight an impending battle, one that has since become regarded as the most heroic and historic action of that Air Force.

But before detailing this battle, it should be recorded that the casualties of the US Army's 32nd Division who, fighting alongside the Australians had erased the Japanese from Buna, numbered more than 10,000.

Casualty evacuation by DC-3s and Lockheed C-60 Lodestars was a prime factor in limiting the death rate to around 7%, an unbelievably low figure for the terrain and type of combat.

Whilst the operation against Buna was being mounted, the 5th Air Force had received its first B-25C Mitchells. But before these went into action, Kenney had insisted they must be modified to make them suited to a strafing rather than a conventional bombing role. Consequently, USAAF engineers in Australia worked day and night to provide them with eight forward-firing machine guns in the nose and fuselage blisters, two 0.5in machine guns in an upper turret, plus the ability to carry up to 60 small fragmentation bombs and six 100lb demolition bombs, or a lesser number of heavier weapons. In the closing weeks of 1942 the 3rd Bombardment Group's 90th Squadron began to perfect a

Top: It was all very well keeping an eye on the enemy, it was more important to have a go at him. The prior need was to build up squadron strength in both men and machines. A B-17E Fortress takes off as it stages through Midway.

Above: The most distinctive B-17 in New Guinea, the only one without camouflage finish, was Kenney's *Sally*, seen here at Port Moresby.

Right: The Douglas A-20 light attack bomber, built originally for the Allies fighting in the European theatre of operations, was to prove a valuable low-level attack aircraft in the Pacific.

Below: Typical of their deployment is this attack against a Japanese base at Kakas, New Guinea. The machine on the right has been hit by enemy anti-aircraft fire.

Bottom: Unfortunately, all new arrivals did not come in one piece. This Douglas B-18A had mixed it with enemy aircraft en route to Hawaii.

new technique for strikes against shipping with these B-25s. In repeated attacks against an old hulk off Port Moresby they had found that direct bombing, using a reference point on the aircraft's nose for aiming, was the most effective. These aircraft were to prove valuable reinforcements in the very near future, deployed with rewarding effect during what has since become known as the battle of the Bismarck Sea.

With the enemy defeated at Buna, and when reconnaissance gave confirmation that the Japanese appeared to regard the area as too costly to hold any longer, there seemed little doubt that special efforts would be made by them to reinforce their garrisons at Lae and Salamaua. Such a course would be vital if New Guinea was to be held as a base from which to mount an offensive against the Australian mainland. Lae and Salamaua were both situated conveniently in the Huon Gulf and within a comparatively short distance of the important base which the Japanese had established at Rabul, creating there its main supply installation for all forces operating in the south and south-west Pacific.

In consequence, the limited efforts of Kenney's only reconnaissance squadron were concentrated to keep close watch on Rabul and the sea lanes leading to the Huon Gulf. As 1942 drew to a close, 5th Air Force Catalinas confirmed that the great harbour at Rabul had accumulated the largest concentration of shipping yet seen there. Furthermore, the activity of enemy reconnaissance aircraft along the sea lanes and in the area of Lae provided reasonable confirmation of the intended direction of this assembly, and all possible steps were taken to provide a worth-

while reception for this convoy should it materialise.

A first minor attempt to reinforce Lae, soon after the beginning of the New Year, was to prove successful, the defending 5th Air Force gaining only limited success against the surface force of about six warships and four transport vessels. There had been no opportunity to launch the low-level attack which had been practised so carefully, but in the air the story was rather better. P-38s and P-40s operating in some strength were able to claim no less than 50 of the enemy's fighter umbrella as being destroyed, for the loss of only 10 of their own number.

It was not until mid-February that intelligence reports suggested the reinforcement of the Huon Gulf installations to be imminent, most likely during the second week of March. While Lae and/or Salamaua were regarded as the most likely goal of the convoy assembling at Rabul, operational plans were drawn up immediately to cater for its dispatch to New Britain via the Dampier Strait, or Madang higher up the New Guinea coast.

The Japanese, however, had no doubts of the importance to them of Lae and Salamaua, and had made very detailed plans to reinforce their troops in this area at almost any cost. Seven transports and eight destroyers, plus the service vessel *Nojima*, were made ready to land a complete infantry division at Lae on 3 March 1943, and this convoy set sail soon after midnight on the first of the month. Initially, the weather favoured the enemy, but a brief sighting between cloud on the morning of 1 March alerted the 5th Air Force to the fact that a 14-vessel convoy was at sea, but that brief glimpse was all that could be

found by way of confirmation on that day. Not until the late morning of 2 March was the convoy's new position established by a patrolling B-24, and immediately a force of B-17s was despatched to 'open the batting'. Although these bombers failed to establish rendezvous with their fighter escort, they pressed on and launched their attack from a height of about 6,000ft (1,830m), scoring hits on three of the transports one of which, the *Kyokusei Maru*, was sunk. About 850 men were rescued from this vessel and, under the cover of darkness, were carried to Lae aboard two of the destroyer escort. They were to prove the sum total of success of this costly reinforcement exercise.

According to captured Japanese documents, no further success was achieved by the 5th Air Force on that day, cloud cover and bad light making it almost impossible to gain more than a fleeting glimpse of their targets, but the morning of 3 March was to prove very different. By then the force was approaching the Huon Gulf, and the shortening range made it possible for Kenney to use the low-level anti-shipping force which had practised so hard to perfect their technique. RAAF Beaufighters led the way, almost skimming the waves as they roared in to the attack, cannons and machine guns blazing, diverting attention from a force of B-17s which launched a simultaneous bombing attack from overhead. Conventionally-armed B-25s followed the Beaufighters, launching a low-level bombing attack. But the most devastating blow came from Kenney's specially-prepared B-25Cs which followed, going in low, each with its eight forward-firing guns blazing to silence any opposition still

Above left: Happily, Gen 'Hap' Arnold's aircraft made a more conventional landing when he paid a visit to Hickam Field, Oahu.

Above: Another of the early, and necessary, morale-raising visits was that of the President's Lady. Eleanor Roosevelt has an informal in-flight chat with M/Sgt Reedy en route to Penrhyn Island, Line Group.

remaining. As they rocketed over the enemy vessels a cascade of 500lb bombs were released, scoring hit after hit, and many of them mortal.

Further strikes were launched during the afternoon, but these were far less effective, their co-ordination and effect destroyed by bad weather which reduced considerably the number of aircraft able to make a concerted attack. Apart from the sinking by bombs of a badly damaged destroyer, on the morning of 4 March, that was the end of the battle. It was to demonstrate most effectively the capability of an air component to isolate and devastate a convoy at sea, without any assistance whatsoever from naval surface units.

Japanese records have since confirmed that as a result of these attacks only four destroyers from the whole convoy survived, the *Asagumo, Shikinami, Uranami* and *Yukikaze*. All of the transports, the service vessel *Nojima*, and the destroyers *Arashio, Asashio, Skikinami* and *Tokitsukaze* were sunk, together with well over 3,000 men. In the air, about 50 of the enemy's air escort were claimed as destroyed: US forces lost one B-17, a B-25 and three P-38s. In later years General MacArthur was to described this as the most decisive aerial engagement in the Pacific theatre. In the same sense that the Doolittle raid on Tokyo had put new heart into the American people, or the Battle of Britain had inspired both civilians and servicemen in the British Isles, this important early success against the might of Japan proved more than a tonic to Kenney's 5th Air Force. Far from home they might be; and inadequately equipped for the enormous task ahead; but no

longer need they regard the Japanese as being invincible.

For the Japanese this action in the Bismarck Sea was a devastating blow. It was made perfectly clear to them that if America and its Allies held air superiority it would prove far too costly to carry men and/or supplies by surface vessels to invade an island or resupply an established garrison. Even more alarming must have been the realisation that at that moment in time, early 1943, American production of military aircraft was nowhere near its peak. No further attempts were made to reinforce Lae or Salamaua.

By the early summer of 1943, Dobodura had been expanded into a major air base, as had been envisaged, providing the essential close-support to eject the Japanese from the Huon Gulf area.

An advance up the coast in mid-March brought the Americans to within 75 miles (121km) of Salamaua, without their meeting any significant opposition on the ground. But the enemy was not insensitive to the advance and began to increase their air activity. There ensued some furious air combats, but as by then the 5th Air Force was able to deploy substantial numbers of the superb Lockheed P-38 Lightning, the Japanese came off by far the worst. Nonetheless, concentration of the fighters to the north of the Owen Stanleys had enabled the enemy to mount two fairly destructive air attacks against Port Moresby.

Preparations for the operations in the Huon Bay area continued on the ground. A battalion was put ashore in Nassau Bay at the end of June, a dicey operation in mountainous surf that deprived the force of most of its equipment. Supplied by air drops, it was

almost two weeks before it could begin a slow advance on Salamaua, a two-pronged attack intended to convince the Japanese that Salamaua was the prime target. The landing force too, was the frequent target of the enemy strafing aircraft, many operating from bases in New Britain, and in a period of eleven days USAAF fighters accounted for 58 fighters and four bombers for the loss of six of their own machines.

With the approach of the Allied forces, new efforts were made by the Japanese to reinforce the defending forces at Lae, largely by barge traffic protected by one or two naval vessels. On 28 July a group of B-25s pounced on two escorting destroyers that had been spotted by a reconnaissance aircraft, and were successful in eliminating both.

Advanced bases to the west and north-west of Lae were needed to contain the enemy, and a strip was prepared at Tsili Tsili, aided by the ubiquitous Douglas C-47s which made the first landings. As the strip extended, more and more 'Gooney Birds' brought in more and more equipment and within about three weeks, 'Silly' could handle up to 150 C-47s a day.

This was a story which was to be retold a thousand times. First came a solitary C-47, trundling into a strip that would have seemed insignificant to a Tiger Moth. The men and equipment aboard made it possible for it to fly out again, leaving them behind to carve out an improved strip that would soon carry increasing numbers of C-47s. Eventually came the moment when they flew off to another site, leaving the new strip for the P-38 Lightnings and Republic P-47 Thunderbolts which spearheaded the Americans in their

Above left: Most urgently requested fighter for the Pacific theatre was the Lockheed P-38 Lightning: fast, hard hitting and able to absorb a lot of punishment. Those which came by sea needed a great deal of preparation before they could be put into service.

Centre left: But the P-38F Lightning, with a top speed of 395mph (636km/h) and armament of one 20mm cannon and four 0.5in machine guns was well worth waiting for.

Bottom left: The P-38F was certainly an all-purpose fighter.

Above: As soon as lines of P-38s began to appear on the airstrips of New Guinea, a genuine *Toryu* (Dragon Killer) had arrived to smite the Japanese.

33

Left: Three B-25s strafe Boram Field (Wewak), New Guinea.

Right: One soon attracted an 'Oscar' of his very own, which he managed to evade . . .

Below: . . . even if the enemy's fire was not too far off target.

Bottom: It was all well worthwhile if several enemy bombers could be left in this condition.

island-to-island advance across the Pacific.

As the north-west base for the attack on Lae, a large, level, grass-covered area known as Nadzab was selected. It, like Dobodura, had potential for expansion as a major air base. It was planned to use a parachute force to take it, linking up later with an Australian force which would foot-slog to the west bank of the Markham River. Simultaneously, an amphibious force would land the Australian 9th Division east of Lae.

In the latter weeks of August the 5th Air Force began to mount relentless attacks on all enemy airstrips in the operational area, and especially the four grouped at Wewak. It was a highly successful exercise, and conservative evaluation of the claims indicates that about 250 enemy aircraft were destroyed in the air or on the ground. When the 'Diggers', some 7,800 strong, were put ashore on 4 September, only a single attack by three bombers was launched against them.

On the following morning, 79 C-47s of the 54th Troop Carrier Wing, with 1,700 paratroopers aboard, made a rendezvous with its 100-strong fighter escort, climbed over the top of the Owen Stanleys, and with clockwork precision unloaded its cargo over Nadzab. Within minutes they had contacted the Australians, who lost little time in crossing the Markham River.

Nadzab fulfilled also its promise as an air base. Just nine days later it possessed two 6,000ft (1,830m) parallel runways and a dispersal area that could handle 36 transports simultaneously.

Above: Unsportingly, the
enemy would retaliate.
Sometimes with spectacular
success, putting this B-24
beyond the miracles that were
often worked by local
maintenance squadrons.

Right: Their endless
nightmare was not maintenance
but repair. This pilot's lucky
escape from heavy flak posed a
major repair problem for a
squadron engineer with few
tools and virtually no spares.

As these forces converged on the Japanese, they met with resistance far less fanatical than that displayed by the defenders of Buna. Unexpected victory came at Salamaua on 13 September, and at Lae three days later.

The rapid fall of these two enemy bases encouraged an early attack on Finschafen at the tip of Cape Cretin, an ideal jump off point for attacks against New Britain. During the night of 21/22 September a naval convoy moved the troops from Lae and around the tip of the Huon Peninsula and, in the early hours of 22 September, they were put ashore at Scarlet Beach, close to the Song River. The landing was virtually unopposed and well over 5,000 troops and their supplies were landed without difficulty.

The main excitement was yet to come. The Japanese had spotted the convoy and, anxious to have a Bismarck Sea victory of their own, despatched large groups of aircraft from New Britain. They had chosen the wrong moment: three fighter squadrons were already patrolling the area and two more were within instant call.

About 30 bombers and 40 fighters flew straight into the trap, which closed relentlessly on 10 bombers and 29 fighters, these falling to the USAAF's fighters, while the Navy's guns accounted for nine more bombers. No damage was suffered by the convoy, and of the three P-38s shot down by the enemy, one pilot was rescued.

Supported by overwhelming air power, the Australian advance on Finschafen progressed much as planned and, 10 days after the landing, the town fell to the 9th Division.

It was not until almost a year later that the Japanese were expelled completely from New Guinea, but enough had been done in 1943 to ensure the safety of Australia, and provide a series of strong bases from which attacks could be mounted on near-by enemy-held islands.

Much had been learnt, and it was clear that the 5th Air Force had a long and arduous task ahead. Slowly but surely the long-range bombers would soften up an island and then, under cover of an air umbrella, would come an amphibious landing. Air support would be maintained, over long range if necessary, until the all-essential airstrip had been captured or created. It was also usual to by-pass non-essential islands in enemy hands

Above: Wheels-up landing of a P-39 means yet another treasure hunt for non-existent spares.

which, isolated from replenishment, could be neutralised subsequently by massive air strikes.

When the Papuan campaign had begun, in July 1942, a landing had also been made at Guadalcanal on the Solomon Islands. It is typical of a different type of operation, based on Navy/Marine Corps landings, with some Air Force assistance, and we shall look closely at this in the next chapter.

Below: Even the collapse of a nosewheel unit on Dobodura airstrip needed hours of work to both engines and airframe before this P-38 was back in the air.

Right: Main sources of treasure were scrap heaps like this. A Liberator well shot up by Japanese 'Zekes' managed to stagger back to base to make this write-off landing. While the carcass was still warm the 'vultures' arrived for their pickings.

3
Guadalcanal to the Central Pacific

Right: One of the greatest of the greats, the ubiquitous, enduring and endearing Douglas C-47. It hauled in anything that could be crammed into its fuselage.

Above: In a somewhat
unsophisticated manner the
C-47 also carried wounded out
of the front line.

Right: In dire emergency a
P-38 could serve as an air
ambulance, with one patient
carried beneath each wing in
modified auxiliary fuel tanks.

In June of 1942 neither the 5th Air Force nor the RAAF could regard its air reconnaissance capability as adequate. Even had there been plenty of aircraft to spare from the task of attempting to confine Japanese expansion, the vast distances involved were still a major headache. Between Port Moresby and Guadalcanal were some 800 miles (1,287km) of open sea, a round trip of 1,600 miles (2,574km). The B-17E, for example, had a still air cruising speed of around 210mph (338km/h) which involved an eight-hour trip at the best.

Nevertheless, it was learned during June that the Japanese were preparing to construct an airfield on Guadalcanal. Reconnaissance confirmed that in early July strong military forces, construction personnel and equipment were being landed near Lunga Point, and it needed no crystal ball to forsee the problems posed. Land-based bombers operating from Guadalcanal would be able to threaten Noumea, New Caledonia, the last vital link in the island chain that maintained the Pacific communication line between Australia and the United States. If the enemy became established there in strength, there was always the danger that he might jump from there to New Caledonia and the New Hebrides. This would not only block the air lanes, but also force the hard-pressed surface transport vessels further south, stretching an already minimal service to breaking point.

Fundamentally a problem for the US Navy and Marine Corps, it was typical of so many similar island stepping stones that needed purification by blood, steel, fire and courage as the Allies moved slowly back towards Japan. But in those early days of the Pacific War, when all of the services were desperately short of men and equipment, it was clear that USAAF help would be essential.

A newly created airstrip on Espiritu Santo Island, New Hebrides, became home to the B-17s of Col LaVerne G. Saunders' Mobile Force, Central Pacific, the first aircraft of which landed there on 30 July 1942. It was not exactly home from home, and for men who had left the sophistication of Hawaii only hours before it must have seemed the end of the world – certainly no idyllic tropical island – as they slept as best they could with only trees for a roof and ate, often meagrely, a monotonous diet of canned food.

Facilities for maintenance and operation of the aircraft were virtually non-existent. Even refuelling was carried out by hand from steel drums, and when you understand that one B-17 with near empty tanks could thirstily guzzle the bucketed contents of 50 drums, you begin to appreciate the nightmare of operating even a minute force under such conditions.

In fact, it proved too much for the first few weeks, until more men arrived, and Saunders elected to operate his force from Efate near the southern end of the New Hebrides, which, established a couple of months earlier, had some semblance of organisation. While it was about 250 miles (402km) further south, full bomb loads could be carried as, in emergency, a landing could be made at Espiritu on the return journey.

On 31 July, nine B-17s made the first strike on Guadalcanal and until the first Marines went ashore, on 7 August, maintained this tempo of attack on a daily basis. Fortunately, the Marines landed against little opposition, as naval guns had put over a fair

Below: In course of time came much improved aero-medical services, such as provided by this Douglas C-54 seen at Funafuti, one of the Ellice Islands.

curtain of steel just prior to their approach to the shore at Lunga Point, where they were able to establish a beachhead.

From then on, Saunders' group was responsible for ensuring that no surprise counter-attack was made on the Marines as they consolidated their beachhead, while Australia-based machines of the 5th Air Force assumed responsibility for reconnaissance north of the island.

It was the latter that reported the approach of an enemy task force on 24 August which, in conjunction with Navy air groups, were hit first on the 24th, and sent packing the following day, during which action the B-17s sank the destroyer *Mutsuki*.

Meanwhile, on the island, the Marines had gained control of the Japanese-initiated airstrip which, on 20 August, received its first US aircraft with the arrival of Marine Corps fighter and Scout/bomber squadrons, VMF-223 and VMSB-232 respectively. They were joined two days later by five P-400s, the advance unit of the 67th Fighter Squadron, the first air force unit to operate from what became known as Henderson Field.

Unfortunately, the P-400s were useless as interceptors and could be used only to strafe Japanese ground forces, who were never very far away. And the enemy soon discovered that if the airstrip was water soaked they were immune from interception, for the Marine's F4F Wildcats could not take-off; the P-400s, which could, were impotent above 12,000ft (3,66om). The enemy took advantage of such conditions, bombing the airstrip by day and sending in surface vessels to shell it by night. Reserves of fuel, ammunition and supplies dwindled, and when morale reached a low ebb it was clear that little more effort would be needed by the Japanese for them to regain control of the airstrip. One of the most

Above left: Disassembled and packaged delivery of short-range aircraft added to maintenance problems in the Pacific. One alternative was to deliver them aboard carriers, like these Republic P-47 Thunderbolts being loaded at Pearl Harbor.

Left: With approach of their destination they were prepared for flight . . .

Top: . . . and were soon roaring off to their new island homes.

Above: An alternative shipboard replenishment system was far more messy. Here we see a North American P-51 Mustang 'airborne' on the first stage of its ship-to-shore journey.

Right: The final stage was even more undignified.

pressing requirements was for first class interceptors. A squadron or two of P-38s would soon eliminate enemy opposition; transports would then have free access to the field and could change the fuel and supplies position overnight. It was a need that clashed with the demands of the Middle East and European theatres. When Maj -Gen Millard F. Harmon, Commanding General of the USAAF, South Pacific Area, expressed the desperate need for such aircraft, he was told in no uncertain terms that his was the lowest priority.

Intervention of the US President, following study of reports from the Pacific, was eventually to resolve this situation, but in the interim period the Japanese began to rush reinforcements to Guadalcanal, using fast destroyers and cruisers that disembarked their troops by night and were away again long before morning.

This replenishment service soon became dubbed the 'Tokyo Express', but without ample aircraft of adequate range there was little that could be done to stop this nocturnal traffic. On the night of 13 October an unusually large force arrived, the naval guns battering Henderson with a furious bombardment that left it a shambles of wrecked aircraft, the airstrip cratered and useless for medium and heavy bombers, and with fuel and ammunition destroyed. By then the Japanese had nearly 30,000 men on the island, and their strength was growing with every passing day.

Vice-Admiral William F. Halsey breathed new life into the situation on October 20, sending in supplies and the 147th Infantry Division, and initiating construction of a second airstrip at Koli Point, 12 miles (19km) from Henderson. It was only just in time, for on 24 October the enemy launched a massive land and air attack on the airstrip and its immediate area. As the issue hung in the balance came news that a powerful Japanese task force was en route, to provide the final thrust that would push the Americans off the island.

So developed the bitter sea-air action known as the Battle of Santa Cruz Islands, during which an enemy battleship and three cruisers were severely damaged and several destroyers sunk for the loss of the uss *Hornet*. On land it was touch-and-go. The defenders at Henderson Field were just able to beat the Japanese attacks; if the reinforcements had got through it would have been the end. By 27 October it seemed as if the situation had been saved.

Once again Air Force reconnaissance aircraft reported another convoy moving towards Guadalcanal, and on 12 November 11 transports protected by cruisers and the battleships *Hiei* and *Kirishima*, the spearhead of a 61 vessel task force, pushed ahead to

46

Medium-range workhorse was the North American B-25 Mitchell (top left). Appropriately named after Billy Mitchell, it soon acquired fame for its low-level attacks on targets of all kinds, ranging from enemy-held bases (above left), to coastal transport vessels (left), and enemy frigates (above), not all of which were clobbered so successfully as this enemy destroyer in Ormoc Bay (right).

renew the attack on the Americans. If they had breached the air and sea defences of Guadalcanal it would have brought a final rout.

Halsey had only the damaged *Enterprise* and a pitifully small force of destroyers and cruisers to meet this attack, but on 12 November air units spread out over a wide area rallied to give their support. By nightfall, Guadalcanal held 41 F4Fs, 30 SBD-3s, 19 Grumman TBF-1 Avengers and two P-400s, as well as eight P-38s of the USAAF's 339th Fighter Squadron. On the following day another eight P-38s from the 39th Fighter Squadron arrived, and B-26s of the 69th and 70th Medium Bomber Squadron flew in to Espiritu.

With these forces battle was joined. Aided by the aircraft flown off *Enterprise* they sank the *Hiei*, and with the B-26s and 17 B-17s from Espiritu throwing in their weight, seven of the transports were destroyed. The remaining four transports reached the island and beached near Tassafaronga, where aircraft and artillery pounded them into smouldering hulks. It remained only for the surface vessels of Rear-Adm Willis A. Lee to sink the *Kirishima* and destruction was complete.

Never again did the Japanese mount such a vast force against Guadalcanal, and although

three more months were to pass before the island was cleared of the enemy, these joint actions in defence of Guadalcanal and New Guinea had cost the enemy dear. The most dangerous moment had passed. From then on Allied strength and reserves were to increase steadily.

Guadalcanal had been a typical Navy/Marine action which gradually, with these initial tentative experiences behind them, grew into a far more sophisticated and predictable, though often costly, exercise. Carriers brought an air umbrella which, together with naval artillery, softened the defences. Then, while Navy and Marine aircraft kept the enemy's heads down, landing craft put the Marines ashore, where they were sustained by the Navy.

In general, the only Air Force participation in such operations was to provide long-range heavy bomber support and, in the early days, long-range reconnaissance. In fact, the reconnaissance sorties over endless miles of featureless ocean made by B-17s of the 5th Air Force were so valuable that it limited their availability as a striking force. High command was not happy at this misuse of the only heavy bombers which were then available in other than penny-packet numbers, but the only alternative available was the Con-

Above: If the B-25's employment was wide ranging, so were their weapons. Everything, including an autographed kitchen sink, was flung at the enemy.

Top right: Repair depots, such as this one operated by the 13th Air Depot Group at Tontouata, New Caledonia, acquired an ever-growing queue of patients.

Above right: Usually, the have-a-go-at-anything low-level B-25J Mitchells formed the major portion of their casualty list.

Right: Even when more modern equipment began to arrive, it was still all-go for the ground crews, for the pitifully small force was only useful when it was airborne. A P-40 is refuelled at Munda Field, New Georgia Island.

solidated PBY Catalina flying boat. While it was an excellent reconnaissance machine, it did not carry the heavy defensive armament of the Fortress, and was vulnerable to the enemy's fighter patrols. The situation was partially resolved when 52 more PBYs were allocated. These were deployed on operations of acceptable risk, supplemented by the B-17s if enemy fighters in quantity were likely to be operating in the search area.

With a steady increase in the number of aircraft available, General Harmon and his staff studied how they could best help to speed up the elimination of the Japanese from their island bases. This led directly to the formation of the 13th Air Force, conceived as a guerilla-type force, and which was established on 5 December 1942. Its general directive in the early days was to gain air superiority and to support land and sea offensives. In conjunction with the 5th Air Force, it made excellent progress in the art, and it was these two forces that were responsible for the devastating attacks on New Britain that led to Japan's loss of Rabaul, its chief supply base in the south and south-west Pacific.

When the Japanese seized New Britain, they gained the established port of Rabaul with seven wharves and protected by two airfields that had been built before the war by the Australians. The docks were expanded and three new airfields were constructed (one across St Georges Channel on nearby New Ireland), so that Rabaul had a protective ring of five airfields.

On this island the Japanese held a six-month inventory of supplies for its army and

Left: Pre-flight checks and rearming of P-40 *Geronimo* of the 45th Fighter Squadron at Nanumea Island, Ellice Islands.

Centre left: Cleaning and maintenance of the rear gun turret of a B-24 Liberator of the 38th Bombardment Squadron (H).

Bottom left: Even making sure that ammunition belts are correctly aligned is something of an anti-Japanese puzzle.

Right: And when you were lucky enough to have a petrol bowser, it was no use raising an eye if its prime-mover seemed a little unconventional.

Below: Camouflage was another chore, but essential while the Japanese fighters were still rampant. The only advantage was that camouflage netting provided a little welcome shade.

Bottom: But on the new strips, the debris of jungle clearance left little room for revetments and camouflage.

naval units operating in the Bismarcks, Solomons and eastern New Guinea areas. For protection of this valuable hoard there was, in addition to the complex of airfields, a strong anti-aircraft defence and early-warning radar that would give at least a 30min warning of impending air attack.

The 5th and 13th Air Forces girded their loins to help in the capture of this important prize. Air reconnaissance on 1 October 1943, had shown 18 naval and 26 merchant vessels in harbour, and later 'looks' accounted for about 125 bombers and 175 fighter aircraft distributed on its airfields.

The attack, planned for 12 October, and which was cited by General Kenney as '. . . the beginning of what I believe is the most decisive action initiated so far in this theatre . . .', began on schedule and B-24s and B-25s with fighter escort, and assisted by RAAF Beaufighters, achieved tactical surprise. While units blasted the airfields, the 90th Bombardment Group struck at the shipping in the harbour. It was a chaotic scene of falling bombs, milling fighters and indiscriminate anti-aircraft fire. Within minutes fires were raging and amidst indescribable confusion vessels were circling the harbour as they attempted to gain the comparative safety of the open sea.

This first raid was a conspicuous success and provisional estimates, later found to be on the conservative side, listed 126 aircraft destroyed, 51 seriously damaged, and heavy destruction of airfield installations and wharves in the harbour. Damage to shipping was not as serious as had been thought from original claims, but any substantial loss of

51

surface transports was a major disaster to the enemy at that stage of the war. On the following day a new attack was mounted, but victory went to the weather, which caused most of the force to abort and claimed four of the fighter escort. Three just disappeared in the limitless grey. One crashed on landing – whipped on its back by a blast of wind of hurricane force.

It was not until 18 October that a new attack in strength was launched; eight squadrons of Liberators and two of B-25s, accompanied by fighter escorts, were once again frustrated by weather conditions that weakened the impact of their attack.

It was typical of the conditions under which these two forces laboured, fighting not only the enemy but the problems of supplies, maintenance, equipment, distance and weather. October passed in this manner but without the attackers being able to maintain continuous pressure the Japanese had time to make good their defences and bring in new equipment.

Air reconnaissance on 1 November showed eight naval and 20 merchant vessels in Rabaul's harbour, and no fewer than 237 aircraft dispersed around its airfields. In clearing weather on 2 November, a force of some 80 B-25s, with a similar number of fighters, were sent off hastily to strike while the iron was hot.

The reception committee was waiting for them, with an intense anti-aircraft barrage supplemented by the guns of every naval vessel in the harbour. In the air were at least 100 interceptors flown by fearless pilots. And when, having run the gauntlet of this initial defence, the Mitchells came in at low-level to strike at the shipping, they were met by a new tactical ploy. Not only were the naval

Left: Preparing a B-24
Liberator for a mission was no
easy task. To start with you
needed quite a few cases of
ammunition for its 10 machine
guns.

Below left: If the mission
included close-support of land
operations the piles of
fragmentation bombs that
needed preparation seemed
endless.

Bottom left: If it came to the
heavy stuff it was certainly no
tropical island picnic.

Below: No less busy were
squadron intelligence officers,
who carefully collected and
collated every scrap of
information that could
conceivably help the success of
any operation.

cruisers and destroyers blasting away at them
with every available anti-aircraft weapon,
they were also discharging their heavy guns
into the harbour, throwing up enormous
sheets of water in the path of the low-flying
attackers. This device accounted for at least
two of the medium bombers. By the time
the Americans had left, some 13,000 tons of
shipping had been sunk and about 80 aircraft
destroyed on the ground or in air combat.
Eight Mitchells and nine P-38s fell to the
enemy.

Day after day the attacks continued,
weather permitting, and by mid-November it
was apparent that for the time being at least,
Rabaul could offer no serious threat to any
Allied operations in that area. This target had
been the combined responsibility of the 5th
and 13th Air Force. They worked in co-
ordination again to hammer the western tip
of New Britain, at Cape Gloucester, which
the Allies needed to take so that they, instead

of the Japanese, could exercise control over
the Vitiaz Strait.

To prepare for an amphibious landing by
the First Marine Division, the Air Forces
began on 13 November to make attacks on
the Cape Gloucester area and the two
Japanese airfields nearby. But it was not
until 18 December that the pressure was stepped up, the 43rd, 90th and 380th Bombardment Groups knocking out both airfields
completely on that day. Day after day they
maintained the pressure, 280 daylight bomber
sorties being flown on Christmas Eve by the
Liberators, while a less intense bombardment
was maintained by night to keep the enemy
without sleep and apprehensive of further
attacks.

There was no let-up on Christmas Day,
the eve of the landing, and some measure of
the Allied support capability at that time is
given by the D-day plan of air cover. It
provided for continuous fighter cover over
the beachhead by one squadron from 0630 to
0700hrs, three squadrons from 0700 to
1400hrs, and a single squadron from 1400 to
1830hrs. By high-level bombing attack,
scheduled for 0700 to 0720hrs, five squadrons
of B-24s were to neutralise all defence
positions adjacent to the landing beach. The
fleet was scheduled to blast the entire area
with a bombardment lasting for 87 minutes
from 0600hrs, followed immediately at
0728hrs by a 15min period during which
three squadrons of Mitchells would ensure
there was no living thing on or near the
beach; a fourth squadron would ring all
landward approaches with a curtain of
phosphorus bombs.

At 0745hrs on 26 December the Marines
went ashore without a shot being fired at
them, and so completely had the area been
saturated by air and sea bombardment that
squadrons of A-20s on air alert were not
needed. At 0900hrs four squadrons of heavies
dropped 1,000lb bombs in the approaches to
the area to eliminate the danger of counter-
attack, and 15min later four squadrons of
medium bombers strafed the coastline east of
the beachhead.

It had been a copy-book exercise and it
was not until mid-afternoon that the enemy
appeared when a force of about 25 Val dive-
bombers, with fighter escort, caught the task
force napping, sinking a destroyer and
damaging several other vessels. But such was
the capability of the air force patrols that 22
of the attacking Vals and 24 fighters were
destroyed. A follow-up attack cost the enemy
16 more aircraft, a rate of attrition they could
not afford.

With the Cape Gloucester beachhead
secure, the Air Force could turn its attention
once again to Rabaul, from where the enemy's
air strikes were being launched. It suffered

Below: A P-40 is the first
arrival at Munda Field, New
Georgia.

Left: First arrival at Makin Islands, Gilberts Group, was this Douglas A-24 being led to its dispersal by a jeep, followed in by a P-39 Airacobra (top) which puts its three feet down neatly on the pierced-steel matting.

Right: Instant ace – nearly – was Lt Murray J. Shubin who scored five confirmed and one probable victory in a brief 45 minutes of action over Guadalcanal.

much the same treatment as had the western tip of the island. By mid April-only about 100 of the 1,400 buildings in Rabaul were still standing and the airfields were in such a state that it was deemed unnecessary to occupy the area.

General MacArthur was later to report to Washington that '. . . the Air Force here has been magnificent and is the very hub of our air success'; and even the one-time anti-air-power Navy described their contribution as superb. In just the same way that the German attack on Coventry had given birth to the word 'Coventrated', the 5th Air Force ever after described a target which had been obliterated as having been 'Gloucesterised'.

One other combat air force had a little finger in most of the pies described so far, namely the 7th Air Force, which had been born out of remnants of the Hawaiian Air Force on 5 February 1942. From 20 June 1942, it was commanded by Maj-Gen Willis H. Hale and, still based on Hawaii, it was in-evitable that its crews became long-range specialists.

General Hale was to comment later that '. . . in our long range operations it was obvious that we could not have fighter cover. On the other hand, flying over these vast expanses of ocean we did not meet a great deal of enemy interception or anti-aircraft fire until we were over the target. To make up for the lack of fighter cover we concentrated on gunnery skill . . .'

First major task of the 7th Air Force was their involvement in the Battle of Midway, their B-17s and B-26s flying well over 1,000 miles (1,610km) out from Hawaii to support Admiral Nimitz's naval forces.

The distances involved meant that many of the 7th's flights required staging posts. This was no great problem if it meant operating through Midway for a combined recon-naissance/bombing attack on Wake Island. It was not so much of a picnic staging some 2,000 miles (3,220km) to Funafuti, in the Ellice Islands, to hit the Japanese airstrip on Tarawa in the Gilberts.

Inevitably, the 7th Air Force crews claimed, with some justification, that their war was just 'one damned island after another'. It would have been an appropriate phrase as a squadron motto for in the monotony of daily patrols over thousands of miles of ocean,

Below: When Guadalcanal was occupied the Japanese watchtower (left) was soon replaced by the somewhat more sophisticated building on the right.

Top right: A Lockheed B-34A takes off from Guadalcanal, a medium bomber developed originally for the British RAF which knew it as the Ventura. Many were withdrawn from Lend-Lease allocations for service in the Pacific, the majority used by the US Navy for overwater patrol duties.

Bottom right: A C-47 of the 6th Troop Carrier Squadron en route from Port Moresby, complete with an escort of P-39s, over the typical wooded and mountainous terrain of New Guinea.

practically all the crews ever saw was islands – islands which differed primarily by being either friendly or hostile.

All planning for a Central Pacific offensive, seeing capture of islands in the Carolines chain as a long but inevitable pathway back to the Philippines, required occupation of the Marshall Islands as as preliminary. But the Marshalls had a protective ring of well fortified enemy positions. It was necessary to maintain thorough reconnaissance and/or air attack on these positions – but how?

It took little time to elect the good-old island-hopping 'Seventh' for the job. Its seven bomber and three fighter squadrons were deployed to Canton and Baker Islands, east of the Gilberts, and the Ellice islands of Funafuti, Nanomea and Nukufetau. Of these, Canton and Funafuti already possessed airstrips that at the latter was 6,600ft (2,010m). But before the other three could become operational, a dense covering of coconut palms had to be removed to permit airstrips and their associated hard standings, revetments and parking areas to be constructed.

The first aircraft began to move into their new bases at the beginning of November 1943, their task to prepare for and support the 27th Infantry Division's landing on Makin on 20 November, and Marine Corps landings on Tarawa and Apamama on 20 and 26 November respectively.

Those crews of the 7th Air Force who had taken part in the early attacks on Tarawa, when based in Hawaii, soon discovered that not only had the Japanese made good the damage caused in those raids, but had also improved their defences. Nevertheless, the B-24s of the 11th Group hit the atoll hard on 13, 14 and 17 November and in co-ordination with strikes from the Navy's carriers on 19 November. But the most important task of the 'Seventh' was to ensure, so far as possible, that the enemy would be unable to offer significant support from the air when the moment came for the inevitable clash of men and arms as the invading troops went ashore. Despite the fact that the Japanese could provide air support from a wide number of bases, in particular from Kwajalein Atoll, the efforts to eliminate air support met with considerable success. Makin was taken in a single day, and the Marines met no opposition at Apamama.

Only at Tarawa, where the major task of immediate pre-landing softening-up had been delegated to bombardment by surface vessels, did the 2nd Marine Corps have a desperate and bloody three-day battle to wipe out the enemy ground forces. Subsequent analysis showed that attack by heavy bombers was superior to the Navy's gunfire for blasting the Japanese infantry out of their fox holes and note taken for future reference.

With the Gilbert Islands back in Allied hands, and as soon as their airstrips were ready to receive the 'Seventh's' aircraft, operations preparatory to the next leap-frog were got under way. This campaign, with the Marshall Islands as the prize, benefited considerably from the new airfields in the Gilberts, enabling the shorter-range aircraft, including A-24s, B-25s and even fighter aircraft to join in the task. Their job was well done, and this enabled the B-24s to concentrate on Ponape on the eastern Carolines, following occupation of Kwajalein and Majuro, completed on 6 February 1944.

Neutralisation of Ponape by the B-24s led to the capture of Eniwetok, the highlight of a period of less than four months in which US forces in the Central Pacific had pushed their bases nearly 2,400 miles (3,860km) west from Pearl Harbor, more than halfway towards the Philippines and the Japanese homeland. By 1 March 1944, they were standing on the most western of the Marshall Islands, ready to advance into Japan's inner defences. It was to be no quick or easy task.

Invasion of Truk, a large triangular atoll whose outer coral reef of 140 miles (225km) circumference encircled well over 200 islands,

Below: Target Rabaul. This important Japanese supply base on New Britain under attack by 13th Air Force B-25s. In the bitter air battles that raged over Rabaul, the Japanese Navy lost nearly 70% of their most experienced naval pilots: a loss that proved irreplaceable.

had been considered as the primary step. Although it was the Japanese headquarters for the central and eastern Carolines, it was found to have indifferent air defences. Thus came the decision to by-pass it, leaving its neutralisation to the heavy bombers of the 7th and 13th Air Forces.

The first of two operations against Truk, night attacks by the 'Seventh's' 30th Bombardment Group, was highly successful catching the enemy on the hop with lights ablaze and anti-aircraft guns unmanned. After the first accurate salvoes of bombs straddled aircraft hangars on Eten Island the lights were quickly doused and frantic but inaccurate fire from the ack-ack lit the night sky. By the time the force turned for home the contents of a large fuel storage tank was adding its glare to the macabre scene.

But it had not been easy. Twenty-two aircraft had set out, staging first from Makin or Apamama to Kwajalein, and nine of their number aborted en-route. The round trip from Kwajalein to Truk was nearly 2,200 miles (3,540km) and those aircraft of the 392nd Squadron had covered some 3,700 miles (5,955km) before regaining their home base at Apamama.

Navigation was critical over such vast ranges, and it is hardly surprising that when the 13th Air Force's 307th Group squadrons made their initial attack against Truk, on 26 March, they were 70 miles (112km) off course. Fuel was by then too low to correct the

error and both squadrons had to return home without bombing their assigned targets. They more than redeemed this 'black' three days later, but the incident is quoted to give some indication of the heartbreaking difficulties involved in the Pacific campaign.

Truk was slowly eliminated from making any significant contribution to the enemy's hard-fought defence of its island bases, but it was not until May 1945 that the Truk Atoll complex ceased to be a constant thorn in the flesh of the US forces. By then the moves to Saipan, Guam and Tinian were at hand, and their later capture led to the establishment of bases from which the 20th Air Force's mighty B-29s would carry 'the whirlwind' to Japan's homeland.

The diminutive 7th Air Force, 'Hale's Handful' as it was known, had played a decisive part in attaining this long fought-after objective.

Top: A conjunction of air and sea power. A squadron of B-25 Mitchells heads out to attack Rabaul while a Navy task force moves towards Cape Gloucester at the other end of New Britain.

Above: P-40 Warhawks at Cape Gloucester. As soon as possible after seizure of the airstrip at Cape Gloucester, short-range attack and fighter aircraft moved in to maintain a no-let-up attack on Japanese-held airfields around Rabaul.

4
The CBI
(China-Burma-India)
Theatre

Left: Under the pressure of attack a DE type frigate founders: note how low the B-26 is making its attacking run in.

From the early days of the Pacific War many uninformed armchair strategists persuaded themselves that China could provide a base from which strikes could be mounted against Japan. If they needed confirmation of their arguments they had to look no further than the celebrated Doolittle raid on Tokyo, in April 1942, which had required the active co-operation of the Chinese. More detailed study at higher level, however, left little doubt that such a policy was impracticable, but the need to help China in her continued resistance to the Japanese was plain for all to see.

First practical air support for the Chinese had come from the American Volunteer Group (AVG) of Brig-Gen. Claire L. Chennault, far better known as the 'Flying Tigers'. Their activities under the leadership of Chennault, a retired Air Corps officer who in 1937 had gone as an adviser to the Chinese Air Force, soon became legendary. In the summer of 1941, some months before the Pacific War erupted at Pearl Harbor, Chennault had been collecting his volunteer pilots at Kunming, together with his pitifully small force of Curtiss P-40s. It comprised initially 100 P-40Bs, the version of the Warhawk with the slowest maximum speed of the series and which was armed with two 0.30in and two 0.50in machine guns. Despite a paper strength of 100 aircraft, the problems of spares, maintenance and repairs meant that it was only on rare occasions that more than 50% of the total was available for operations.

We have already learned of the limitations of these aircraft, and no one was more aware of them than the AVG's commander. In order to minimise their disadvantages, Chennault indoctrinated his pilots with the almost unbreakable rule that the enemy must be forced to fight on the 'Tigers'' terms: at those heights and speeds and tactical conditions which enabled the P-40 to operate at its optimum performance.

It was a plan of campaign that paid off. In their first action on 20 December 1941, the AVG destroyed six enemy aircraft without loss. By the time they ceased to exist as an independent group, on 4 July 1942, they had accounted for 286 Japanese aircraft for the loss of only 23 of their own pilots.

The AVG's primary task was to defend the Burma Road, a constant target for the Japanese, and their efforts were such that not only did they take a worthwhile toll of the enemy's men and aircraft, they also helped to ensure that a constant trickle of supplies got through to the Chinese from Burma. More significant, perhaps, was the psychological effect on their ally, who was getting real aid at last rather than promises of it.

There was no doubt that the Chinese needed some positive support as, apart from the

somewhat frail lifeline of the Burma Road, they were virtually isolated. It could be argued that the enemy's 4,000 mile (6,440km) line of communication between Burma and Japan was equally vulnerable. Under normal circumstances this would have been true. But because of their occupation of lands or islands, the Japanese firmly controlled the surface routes and their supply lines were vulnerable only to air attack, of which in the early days of the war there was no threat because the Allies did not have aircraft suitable for the task.

To help resolve some of the problems in the CBI theatre, the 10th Air Force was created on 12 February 1942, and placed under the command of Maj-Gen Lewis H. Brereton. Its nucleus was the 7th Bombardment Group, which had been en-route to the Philippines at the outbreak of war, was diverted to Australia, and finally arrived at Karachi, India, on 12 March. To it was added the 'might' of the 51st Fighter Group which landed up in Karachi at about the same time, complete with its ten rather worn-out P-40s.

This meagre force had hardly found time to become familiar with the surroundings before a crisis in the Middle East sent Brereton scurrying to that theatre, taking with him all available heavy bombers, transport aircraft and personnel. To Brereton's chief of staff, Brig-Gen Earl L. Naiden, fell the unenviable task of building up the force again but he had barely started the job when Brig-Gen Clayton L. Bissell assumed command in mid-August.

Bissell's first job was to create some organisation out of the chaotic conditions then

Above: In China, the American Volunteer Group (AVG) under the leadership of Maj-Gen Claire L. Chennault offered virtually the only opposition to the Japanese who mounted constant attacks against the 'Hump' supply route. Chennault is seen inspecting one of the slit-trench observation posts which was their early-warning system of enemy attack.

Above right: When the China Air Task Force (CATF) succeeded the AVG, this line-up of P-40s represented the major portion of its fighter strength.

Right: Pilots of the P-40s that fought the enemy over China needed a super abundance of confidence. Confidence that they were superior to the enemy, as well as confidence in their aircraft, for they were operating over some of the world's most inhospitable terrain.

existing. An Indian Air Task Force (IATF) was established under Col Caleb V. Haynes, and a China Air Task Force (CATF) commanded by Brig-Gen Chennault, who had been recalled to active Air Force duty in April 1942. His gallant AVG became integrated into the USAAF.

First priority on Bissel's brief was to ensure the continuity of air supplies for China and the CATF, over the 'Hump' of the Himalayas to Kunming. The withdrawal of the transport aircraft to the Middle East had endangered an already minimal flow restricted to the most vital supplies. By giving transport aircraft first call on maintenance and by using every available aircraft he stopped the downward trend. But a great problem was the lack of airfields in China, and this involved a great deal of lost time while slow-moving negotiations for new ones were completed with Generalissimo Chiang Kai-shek. Then, just as Bissel's efforts were beginning to show dividends, responsibility for the continuance of this task went to a newly formed Air Transport Command.

The 10th Air Force, relieved of this exhausting airlift, was by no means out of work and, as the end of the monsoon season was approaching, there seemed every likelihood of a strong upsurge in enemy air activity. The assumption was correct. On 25 October 1942, the Japanese struck the first damaging blow on Assam. The most severe loss was that of five transport and seven fighter aircraft destroyed on the ground and four more transports and 13 fighters damaged. The attack, by a force of about 100 aircraft, also caused considerable damage to runways and buildings.

Two other, less successful, raids were made during October, but by the first days of November the offensive strength of the 10th Air Force was beginning to build up. When they took the initiative, mounting regular attacks on Rangoon and beginning operations against the railway marshalling yards at Mandalay, the Japanese found that their aircraft were then needed for defence rather then attack.

It was inevitable that Rangoon should be the number one target. As the principal port it was host to some 30,000 tons of shipping in early 1943. Aviation fuel represented a large proportion of this tonnage and cutting it off would have an immediate effect on the enemy's military operations. To supplement conventional air attack on such an important target, a number of Liberators were modified to carry magnetic mines and for the remainder of 1943 mine-laying operations were to be a regular feature of the 10th Air Force's commitments.

Reduction of supplies through Rangoon was augmented by regular and damaging

attacks on the long road and rail routes stretching north to Myitkyina and Lashio. When B-24s destroyed a large oil refinery at Bangkok a curtailment of Japanese attacks seemed inevitable. Unfortunately, these activities coincided with the onset of the monsoon season, which reduced Allied air activity and gave the enemy breathing space.

The year of 1943 started well when, in early January, the Myitnge rail bridge was destroyed by air attack. This severed rail communications south of Mandalay and despite the most strenuous attempts at reconstruction, the bridge was never again entirely serviceable. Maintaining the advantage gained by this success the 'Tenth' concentrated their efforts against military installations and communication routes in the northern areas. When, in November, it was decided to make an all-out attempt to neutralise Rangoon, a B-25 group belonging to the 5th Air Force (European theatre) was called in to give assistance. Four strikes by the combined force of B-24s and B-25s sufficed to cripple the dock installations and railway marshalling yards, reducing incoming supplies to a trickle. The 10th Air Force had at that time gained air superiority over most of the country and was able to turn its attention to supporting the ground offensive in Northern Burma.

Following the strategy inspired by the British Maj-Gen Orde Wingate, a First Air Commando Force had been organised and it, in conjunction with the 10th Air Force's Troop Carrier Command, was detailed to mount an attack at the rear of the Japanese positions, far east of the Burma border. Air Commando gliders, towed by transport aircraft carrying a picked division of Wingate's troops, would land at three selected sites, designated 'Broadway', 'Chowringhee' and 'Piccadilly'. There, airborne engineers would build airfields with equipment brought in by the gliders, while Wingate's Chindits would provide protection from surprise attack. Once the airfields were operational, transport aircraft would fly in troops.

Wingate's approach to this kind of operation demanded the preservation of the utmost secrecy, to ensure that the area chosen for occupation was taken completely by surprise. This meant that he objected strongly to both reconnaissance or tactical flights in the immediate vicinity and hence preparations for the airborne attack had to be made with no up-to-the-minute knowledge of the situation in the landing zones. At the eleventh hour, and without Wingate's consent, a reconnaissance sortie was made, and discovered that 'Piccadilly' had been liberally covered with large tree trunks to prevent aircraft from landing there. Accordingly it was decided to land all the gliders on 'Broadway', and on the night of 5 March a total of 67 Waco CG-4As were despatched. Of this total only 32 reached the assigned zone, and of these only three survived the landing in a condition that would allow them to be towed out again. Thirty-one men were killed and 30 injured as the gliders came in to land on a surface that was criss-crossed with ditches and which ripped the landing gear from the first machines to put down. This prevented them being removed and the next group to land crashed into them.

But despite the chaos, more then 500 men survived, together with close on 30 tons of equipment, which included bulldozers. Within 24 hours they had prepared a workable airstrip and the C-47s began an almost continuous shuttle service which, in five days, brought in over 9,000 men, mules and some 250 tons of equipment and supplies. 'Chowringhee' witnessed a smaller and more orderly arrival of airborne forces on the night of 6 March.

The 'Tenth's' Troop Carrier Command then had the responsibility of maintaining this force by air drop, a formidable task indeed, for they advanced in 26 columns of 300 to 400 men, spread out over a steadily widening area. In six days the 27th Squadron dropped over 360 tons of supplies and in the period 20 March to 5 April the same squadron, aided by the US 315th Squadron and No 117 Squadron RAF, dropped no fewer than 850 tons.

The primary aim of the expedition was to isolate the Japanese 18th Division, which would have had the effect of eliminating enemy resistance in Burma within a short period of time. But the expedition failed to achieve its objective and the enemy was able to concentrate his defences at Myitkyina.

Left: Lt-Gen 'Hap' Arnold visits Kunming to see the handful of men and machines that were scoring so heavily against an air force that was numerically far superior.

Above: Battle flag of the Flying Tigers (AVG), designed at the Walt Disney studios in 1943. Although they were then a part of the 14th Air Force, these pilots still retained great pride in the original AVG and its achievements.

Almost simultaneously with the Wingate operation, the Japanese struck at the British positions at Imphal and immediately this increased enormously the responsibilities of Troop Carrier Command. In addition to its other tasks the Command now had to maintain full air supply to a mixed force of 58,000 British and Indian troops for almost three months.

These operations were typical of those needed to break the enemy's hold on Burma, but demanded such an enormous effort from the 10th Air Force that it was impossible for them to assist in the very desirable aim of expanding American air strength in China. In early 1943 the force operating in China had, as a result of an acute shortage of supplies and fuel been reduced to providing little more than token assistance to the Chinese. Thus came the decision to activate the 14th Air Force. Although the intent was good, however, it was to comprise only one heavy and one medium bomber and four fighter squadrons, plus a photo-reconnaissance unit until the late summer of 1943.

The first attacks by the 14th Air Force's 308th Bombardment Group of Liberators were made against Haiphong and Sama Bay on 4 May 1943, that on the latter target proving a distinct success. Four days later another attack was launched against Tien Ho aerodrome at Canton, where considerable damage was caused and 13 enemy fighters were destroyed in air combat. At this point the main logistic problems of these operations were pinpointed. Stocks of fuel, ammunition and bombs were inadequate for further attacks, and the B-24s had to be used in a transport role, operating over the Hump, to build up supplies before they could continue their offensive operations.

This was typical of the problem which was to be the biggest headache of the commander of the 14th Air Force, General Chennault. Restricted in operational scope because of his comparatively small force of aircraft he suffered further limitations as the acute shortage of fuel often meant that even in desperate situations only a percentage of available aircraft could be deployed. When small numbers of P-38s began to arrive to replace the inadequate P-40s, the latter aircraft were regarded as the more valuable of the two since their fuel consumption per sortie was considerably lower. When the Japanese made a final all-out effort in China, seeking to establish an unbroken transport route from Korea to French Indo-China and, at the same time, to overrun the 14th Air Force's foward bases, stocks were so critical that fuel was virtually reserved for the fighters. The bombers were thus relegated to a transport role, ferrying fuel and ammunition over the Hump. Even these supplies proved

inadequate, and fighter operations often had to be stringently controlled. The fact that in early January 1945 the bases at Kanchow and Suichow held fuel stocks of only 400gal (1,500 litres) and 950gal (3,550 litres) respectively illustrates how critical the situation had become.

Despite this frustrating situation the 'Fourteenth' continued to make life difficult for the enemy, to an extent that Japanese officers from the Chinese theatre were to comment after the war's end that, but for the 14th Air Force: '. . . we could have gone anywhere we wished'.

The situation in Burma was far easier as the 10th Air Force did not suffer from the same shortage of supplies – which was just as well for the forces attempting to dislodge the enemy from Myitkyina. There, towards the end of April 1944, a special effort was made to relieve the besieged town by means of a three-pronged attack. The most crucial of these attacks was a surprise advance over the Kumon range of mountains to be made by a special force known as Merrill's Maurauders supported by units of the Chinese 50th Division.

The Maurauders were considered an elite combat force and were some 3,000 strong comprising selected well-trained troops. They included in their ranks veterans of Guadalcanal and men of the Caribbean Defense Command in about equal proportions. Their attack on 17 May met with initial success, but confusion in flying in suitable reinforcements,

Above: Main supply line for the Japanese fighting in the CBI theatre was the long sea lane to the home islands. Allied air power concentrated on breaking this line, attacking constantly the cargo vessels and their attendant frigates. Here a DE type frigate comes under attack from B-25s of the 'Air Apache Group'.

Above right: Eventually the boot changed from the Japanese to Allied foot. As the first Boeing B-29 Superfortresses began to operate out of bases in India their immense weapon loads began to blast Japanese-held towns and positions.

Right: They were operations that, in the final analysis, so often left the pitiful problem of the parentless refugees.

panic amongst the inexperienced Chinese troops, and the falling morale of Merrill's Maurauders, enabled the Japanese to maintain their hold on Myitkyina.

Once again it fell to the 'Tenth' to bring in supplies and reinforcements and, by superb close-support operations, to make good the situation caused by an acute deficiency of artillery weapons. These latter operations were made particularly difficult by the dense jungle which prevented easy designation of the targets. The old and tried system of ground panels proved useless in such terrain and smoke shells were, for various reasons, insufficiently accurate. A system employing a transparent plastic grid that could be used to overlay reconnaissance photographs of enemy-held areas was developed. Using the co-ordinates inscribed on the grid, ground units could call for strikes on easily pinpointed positions. As experience was gained the system worked well, but inevitably increased the 'Tenth's' workload, requiring reconnaissance and close-support missions galore in addition to the delivery of ammunition, equipment, supplies and reinforcements and the evacuation of casualties.

Between 17 May and 3 August 1944, when Myitkyina finally fell to the Allies, over 2,500 sorties had been flown by the close-support fighter/bombers. This was a remarkable achievement during the monsoon season when apalling weather conditions regularly restricted such operations to a few hours per day. There was no doubt that air power had made possible the capture of this important enemy stronghold, but it was almost two months before the Allies were able to renew their offensive.

With this new drive to eliminate the Japanese from northern Burma, the 'Tenth' was extended to its maximum, delivering nearly 212,000 tons of cargo and almost a quarter of a million men to forward areas, maintaining close-support and interdiction operations at an ever-increasing tempo. Then, in preparation for an attempt to take Rangoon, gun emplacements and troop concentrations within the area were subjected to an almost continuous pounding from the air in a period of six days beginning on 26 April. On 3 May 1945, Allied troops entered the city without opposition and at that moment, for all practical purposes, Burma was liberated.

Capture of Myitkyina had enabled US engineers to develop it into a valuable air base, and a fuel pipeline from Tingkawk Sakan to the growing airfield was completed at the end of September 1944. This was of considerable help in the impending campaign to break the Japanese hold on China.

When, on 31 October 1944, Lt-Gen Albert C. Wedemeyer replaced Gen Stilwell as chief of staff to Generalissimo Chiang Kai-shek and as Commanding General, United States Forces in the China Theatre, he faced some formidable problems, especially those posed by the Japanese drive towards French Indo-China which had begun four months earlier.

As the Japanese had advanced, meeting little determined resistance on the ground from ill-equipped and poorly-trained Chinese forces, the only serious threat to their advance was that offered by the 14th Air Force. Consequently, every effort had been made by the enemy to deprive the 'Fourteenth' of its forward air bases. In this it had been successful especially as lack of supplies, particularly of fuel, had limited the extent to which the Air Force was able to retaliate.

Thus Chennault lost many of his hard-won bases and within two weeks of Wedemeyer's arrival Liuchow was taken. With columns advancing south-west from Luichow and north-west from Canton, it was clear that the base at Nanning was next in line for attack and this fell on 24 November. All the major Chinese airfields were now in Japanese hands.

The new commander could plan only on a holding action until May 1945, when he hoped he would have built up the strength of his combined forces for an all-out attack. But, as we shall see in later chapters, the long-range Boeing B-29 Superfortresses of the XXth Bomber Command had entered service by then and had reached bases in southern Bengal. From there, commanded by Maj-Gen Curtis E. LeMay from 29 August 1944, they

had carried out their first combat operations.

The potential of these VHBs (Very Heavy Bombers), as they were known initially, was such that it was inevitable that Chennault, through Wedemeyer, should ask for their assistance to check the Japanese advance through China. Gen LeMay, already committed to a heavy programme, was reluctant at first to comply, but later agreed to provide some limited assistance.

Plans were developed to launch a heavy strike against Hankow, vital supply base for the Japanese forces which then seemed to be heading for Kunmig, the eastern terminus of the Hump route. The proposal was that the B-29s would make a daylight incendiary raid and that, in the post-attack confusion, the 'Fourteenth' should use their available units to rake over the ashes and keep the fires going.

The plan was put into operation on 18 December when 94 of the huge B-29s set out for the target. Unfortunately, a late request to advance the action by 45 minutes was not received by the 40th Group and the complicated scheme of the operation went astray. When the latter group arrived over Hankow billowing smoke hid its targets from view. But despite this miscarriage of the original plan, 40 to 50% of the city was wiped out in a single strike, eliminating it as a major base for the enemy.

It was very different to the 'big shows' mounted by the 'Fourteenth', when anything between 10 and 20 aircraft represented a major effort. Nonetheless, by subtle use of his small force, Chennault succeeded in outfoxing the enemy time and time again. Decoy strikes in more remote areas kept the enemy guessing, making him move troops and aircraft from one place to another to meet a possible threat and as a result diluting the main thrust to the west.

In February 1945 all available aircraft were

Above: Flying out from the Indian and advanced Chinese bases, 14th Air Force aircraft began to reconnoitre the way back to the Philippines. Taken on 12 May 1944, this was the first look at Corregidor since American and Filippino troops had been forced to surrender in 1942.

employed in a programme of interdiction that slammed hard at transport of every kind and sought to eliminate any bridges whose removal could conceivably hamper movement by the enemy. By the end of the month nearly 150 locomotives had been destroyed and even larger numbers had been rendered incapable of puffing their way over hastily repaired and often hazardous tracks. When the Japanese hauled them away to repair depots such concentrations were battered into uselessness by the Liberators of the 308th Bombardment Group. These Liberators were, however, withdrawn for use on the 'Hump' route late in March 1945.

The task of the remaining fighter/bombers was therefore all the greater, but there was the ever constant problem of inadequate fuel supplies. Former free-ranging activites were confined to carefully detailed targets so that the maximum effect could be achieved by a minimum force. But despite these restrictions the 14th Air Force continued to make itself something more than a nuisance. In its close and accurate support of the Chinese ground forces it imbued them with a new confidence and this resulted in their earlier weak resistance to Japanese attack suddenly blossoming into a stubborn defence.

In April the enemy began a new major offensive with some 60,000 troops. They were opposed by nearly 100,000 Chinese but in earlier confrontations such numerical superiority had meant little. This time it was different, for Lt-Gen Wedemeyer had made use of the winter months to regroup and re-equip the Chinese and had flown their Sixth Army out to Burma for training. When they were flown back, in time to meet this new offensive, they had learned many new techniques.

One of the most valuable was that of employing to maximum advantage the close-support that could be provided by the 'Fourteenth's' fighter/bombers. Eight ground-air liaison teams had been taught the importance of maintaining close contact with the enemy so that they could acquire the best targets for their supporting aircraft. As this technique was seen to be hitting and hurting the enemy, Chinese morale improved by leaps and bounds. It became the turn of the Japanese to seek safety by digging-in, which availed them of little more than sudden and unpleasant death. The liaison groups called for napalm strikes against such positions and as the searing flames flushed the Japanese from their hides they were wiped out by concentrated small arms fire.

By mid-May the Chinese had the upper hand. As the Japanese beat a retreat down the Hsiang Valley, they were speeded by the 5th Fighter Group which urged them along by generous doses of machine gun fire. The retreat signalled a general Japanese withdrawal from China. As May neared its end they were seen to be moving back towards the Indo-China border and a month later their strongly held positions along the coast, near Shanghai, were evacuated. By the end of July central China and the coastal areas were virtually free of the enemy and with Japan's surrender in August the seemingly intermidable Sino-Japanese conflict finally ended.

The liberation of China had come, to a very great extent, from air power. Not only had allied airmen fought and died in combat, in attacks on heavily defended targets, or been lost among the hostile peaks of the Himalayas, they had by their unrelenting efforts maintained the all-important supply route over the Hump. It was a victory to which the 'Fourteenth' had made a significant contribution: a contribution that one of Chennault's group commanders described appropriately as 'the mostest with the leastest'.

Above: Meanwhile, B-24 Liberators of the 5th Air Force mauled the enemy. In this attack on a Japanese airfield at Hollandia, New Guinea, a total of 189 enemy aircraft were claimed destroyed on the ground.

5
Men,
Machines and
Maintenance

Left: Practically every island around New Guinea held a
Japanese airstrip which had to be wiped out. Wake Island
receives a visit from the B-25s.

The war in the Pacific theatre of operations is one that is difficult to describe chronologically or in detail, except at considerable length. It is even more difficult to examine in isolation the contribution of the USAAF, operating as it did in conjunction with its own Army on the ground, as well as with the US Navy and Marine Corps, and the land, sea and air forces of America's Allies. But the greatest problem in bringing the story of this air force to life is posed by the location of the vast arena in which its battles were fought: one so far removed from both America and Britain that, by and large, the citizens of these nations were unable to appreciate the bitterness and horrors of the conflict.

I would like to try to depict more clearly the courage and determination of the men who fought this remote war often, with some justification, believing themselves to be forgotten. They battled not only against the fanatical determination of the Japanese, but had to contend also with the enemy's trinity of allies: climate, distance and terrain.

It was inevitable that the problems should seem so much worse in the early days of the war. Then, lack of experience was not limited to the rawest recruit, but stretched all the way to the top brass. The reason was that a completely new kind of warfare was evolving, breaking away from the traditional conflict in which large land armies had been locked in direct confrontation. In the beginning, too, the remnants of those units which had survived the initial eruption of the Japanese forces over the face of the Pacific, were suf-

fering from a extremely low state of morale. This was not surprising, for the decimated regiments and squadrons who found a haven in northern Australia – men rescued from the Philippines and Java – were already war weary. They lived under primitive conditions, eating from tins, lacked even the most elementary resources, were desperately short of arms and ammunition, and were without any kind of recreation. It is to their credit that these men and their leaders succeeded in regaining the confidence to face what must have seemed a hopeless fight.

As an example, the men of Col Saunders' 11th Bombardment Group who were based on Espiritu Santo at the end of July 1942 were faced from the outset with heartbreaking conditions. Even the most primitive living accommodation was nonexistent: it was a case of sleep in or under your aircraft, or rely upon the palm trees to provide sufficient cover. A very limited variety of canned food made up the monotonous diet that became more unsatisfying with every passing day. This was about the sum total of the credit balance.

On the debit side there was a complete absence of ground personnel, which meant that the flight crews had to service, arm and refuel their own aircraft. The latter was a Herculean task, for with no docks, roads or unloading facilities, drums of fuel were dumped overboard from the fleet transports, floated ashore and had to be manhandled to the airstrip. To use the fuel meant more backbreaking work, rolling the drums up a ramp so that their contents could be poured

Above: Inevitably it came the turn of the Americans to hold New Guinea bases, from where to build up their strength for the next jump. This line up of North American B-25s on Mar Strip, New Guinea, are readied for action against enemy held bases in the nearby Halmaheras and Celebes.

Right: A 13th Air Force Liberator over the Japanese-held island of Biak, in the Schouten Group, west of New Guinea.

Above right: Consolidated B-24s of the 26th Bomb Squadron, 11th Bombardment Group, set out to attack Wake Island on 30 April 1944.

into small-capacity manual bowsers. In an emergency this was too slow and on more than one occasion every airman at Espiritu helped form a bucket line of fuel to slake the thirst of the B-17s.

Under such conditions it could hardly be expected that aircraft and their near-exhausted crews should be 100% efficient, yet there were those who criticised their operational achievements. Saunders listed for the doubters some of the contributory factors for his Group's apparent lack of punch. It included minimal maintenance, no relief crews, innaccurate intelligence reports, the inability to carry out a training programme because of fuel shortages and the limited availability of every essential spare, inadequate maintenance of bombsights and instruments and the never ending problem of unpredictable weather and flights over extreme ranges.

Poor maintenance and long-range operations played havoc with the engines of the B-17s upon which so much depended in 1942. Not only were new engines in short supply, but those that did arrive often could not be unloaded from the ocean transports. Thoughtless loading at US ports had placed heavy deck cargoes aboard that were beyond the lifting capacity of the ship's cargo booms. The result was that at Espiritu and other islands some vessels lay offshore for periods of up to three months before they could be unloaded.

Even when cargo holds were not clamped down by some oversize piece of equipment, it was still something of a problem to locate

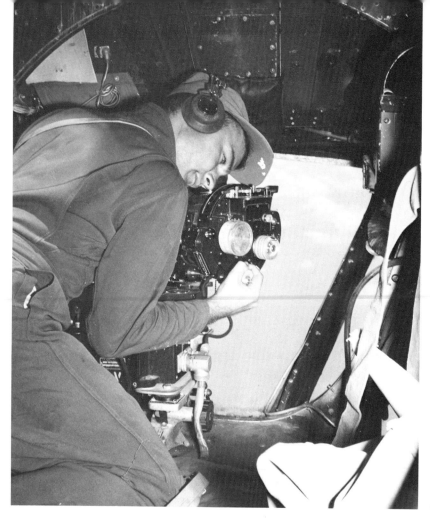

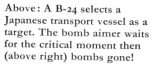

Above: A B-24 selects a Japanese transport vessel as a target. The bomb aimer waits for the critical moment then (above right) bombs gone!

an urgently needed case of spares, for documentation of the ship's cargo was inadequate. Top priority went to replacement aircraft and vessels were invariably relieved of these without delay: but then the ship would be turned back to its former anchorage for complete unloading at a more convenient moment, taking with it the spares and essential equipment for the machines already unloaded.

But even assuming the best – that you had received your precious cargo of aircraft in one piece, complete with all essential equipment, armament and spares – was it really what you needed for the job? This was one of the major problems that faced Gen Harmon in these early stages of the war. The B-17 Flying Fortress, so named to emphasise its heavy defensive armament, was found to be wanting when faced by frontal attack from the Japanese Zero fighters.

Modification of the B-17s was requested to provide two fixed forward-firing 0.5in machine guns in the nose, another in the radio compartment, as well as improved mounts and larger ammunition boxes for the waist guns. Col Saunders was convinced that only a power operated forward-firing turret would prove effective, but this was beyond the capability of Australian-based modification facilities at that time. It was not until B-17Gs appeared, at the end of 1943, that this desirable feature became standard.

The Consolidated B-24 Liberators arriving in the theatre were found to suffer a similar deficiency in fire power. This was overcome in the field by obtaining and fitting in the nose standard Consolidated tail turrets which carried two 0.5in machine guns. Kenney's B-24Ds also had a retractable ventral ball turret mounting two 0.5in guns which he required to be replaced by two manually operated guns.

Such modifications carried out in the Pacific operational zone represented a major operation and to prevent overloading of limited theatre facilities it was desirable that they should be carried out during construction. Unfortunately, this posed new problems for the manufacturer, as at the time these requirements differed from those of other theatres. Eventually it was found that the proposed revision of the Liberator represented an armament improvement for operations anywhere, but it was not until the B-24G appeared in early 1943 that an upper nose turret became standard equipment.

This particular type of problem for the manufacturer was to rear its head again and again. The requirements of the short/medium-range operations of the European and Middle East theatres often differed quite considerably from those needed for the long ranges of the Pacific. This meant that maximum output which required standardisation had to be sacrificed in the interest of specialist requirements – a thing never popular with manufacturers.

Typical of an aircraft that differed quite considerably in its specification for operations in the European and Pacific theatres was the North American B-25 Mitchell. B-25Cs and Ds had proved valuable additions to Kenney's striking power but he had doubts about the B-25G. This type mounted in the nose one of the heaviest pieces of airborne artillery of World War II, a standard Army 75mm field gun. Reserving the right to modify them if they were found to have deficiencies in operations, Kenney expressed his real interest in the proposed B-25H, which would carry an improved 75mm gun and no fewer than 14 0.5in machine guns, as well as the B-25J which was not so heavily armed. The former he wanted for strafing missions, the latter as a bomber.

Then came news that the B-25H, to meet the requirements of the European theatre, would have no co-pilot's position and would lose two guns to accommodate a cabin heater. Kenney's machines certainly didn't need heaters, especially at the expense of a co-pilot who was considered indispensable for low-level attack, and he protested strongly. Again AAF Headquarters and the manufacturer had to go into a huddle.

When Kenney received his B-25Gs it was realised quickly that whilst the 75mm cannon was an excellent offensive weapon, especially against enemy shipping, there was inadequate forward-firing defensive armament. The local maintenance units got to work to provide four extra forward-firing guns, but their initial efforts were not crowned with success. After a comparatively small number of rounds had been fired both primary and secondary structures showed signs of damage. Australian-based facilities finally solved the problem by 'beefing up' the structure.

When the B-25J entered service in the Pacific during 1944 it, too, was handed over to the 'mod' boys, giving it a 'solid' nose carrying eight foward-firing guns. This subsequently became standard production armament and when, later, eight 5in rocket projectiles were carried on under-wing racks, the B-25J proved to be one of the most formidable attack bombers of the war.

But in the early months of the war the day-to-day maintenance and repair of the small and overworked fleet of aircraft was little short of an engineer's nightmare. The rough airstrips knocked hell out of the landing gear and tyres, and shook up the rest of the structure. Hours of flight in tropical storms proved too much for both engines and airframes; torrential rain stripped the fabric used

Below: A direct hit on the 5,000 ton vessel.

Below: Some had the luck, this B-17 at Hickham Field had completed 200 missions.

to seal fairings and inspection panels, and then seeped in to create havoc with electrical systems.

Electrical equipment soon acquired a highly-corrosive fungoid growth and external metal surfaces, rapidly stripped of protective paint by the combined action of heat and the sharp precipitation of tropical storms, corroded almost immediately. And remember too that there were at first few spares, only elementary tools – and the Japanese!

The last, in a most unsportsmanlike manner, kept damaging these precious aircraft, requiring that they should be repaired with nonexistent materials. A badly-damaged and unrepairable machine that succeeded in regaining its base was at once a serious loss and a Godsend. A Godsend because serviceable components stripped from it, or sections of its light alloy skin, could be used to get other machines back into the air. Even tin cans were carefully saved, cut and flattened, so that they could be used to patch bullet holes in skin and control surfaces.

Like Oliver Twist, the flying units wanted more; more aircraft, spares, engines, tools, men, fuel and equipment. Often the first item proved particularly disappointing, for new aircraft could not often be put into use immediately.

One of these reasons, as we have already seen, was modification to theatre requirements. There were others too, such as the receipt of aircraft built for cold-weather operations during the European winter, which arrived in the south Pacific complete with winterisation equipment. All of this had to be removed by the pitifully small labour force before the aircraft could be used on operations.

Another great disappointment followed the arrival of the first frequently demanded P-38 Lightnings. About 60 had arrived in October 1942. but all suffered from leaking fuel tanks and needed in addition various permutations of major repair or adjustment to armament, electrical inverters, engine superchargers and coolant radiators. It took three months before they were able to be used in any significant quantity.

Good fortune or great foresight must have positioned Gen Kenney in the right place at the right time, for he was a highly skilled Air Force engineer. Experience had given him the knowledge and confidence to know when and when not to extemporise and he was always keen to find short cuts if they were sound engineering practice. But although his understanding enabled him to offer many

Left: Some didn't. Funeral service for a USAAF pilot killed in action at Funafuti Island, Ellice Islands.

suggestions that were to keep tired aeroplanes in the air in the opening rounds of the fight, it was clear to him that a major maintenance facility in a forward area was essential.

Accordingly, in early 1943, a new air depot was opened at Townsville on the Australian mainland, some 600 miles (965km) from the important Allied base at Port Moresby. Consisting initially of 16 hangars to provide space for aircraft repair and overhaul, as well as warehousing, it was built largely by American servicemen. But 600 miles from Moresby was a long way at that time and it was decided that the 27th Air Depot Group based at Brisbane should be moved into the front line to help ease aircraft maintenance problems.

Their move in itself is interesting, for it gives some idea of the hardships faced by men in the forward areas. They arrived by sea at Moresby and disembarked into waiting trucks. The more naive might have imagined that this was the first well organised step to convey them to an established base camp. They were soon disillusioned. Carried some seven miles (11km) into a region that became progressively more desolate, they were left in an area of waist-high kunai grass, the home of untold millions of mosquitoes. Their 'well established' base camp was carried in the field packs on their backs. The only water supply immediately available was that in their canteens and it was not until other stores and equipment began to arrive from Moresby that the most elementary field kitchen could be set up.

Amongst the last equipment to arrive was one small case labelled 'Carpenter's Kit'. With the tools therein the 900 or more men were expected to clear the site, construct and erect

the buildings necessary to establish a base camp.

As you might expect, they succeeded. And when buildings were required to house sheet metal workers, welding gear and machine tools they built those too. Almost within no time it seemed as if they had always been there as, enthusiastically, they joined in the then-current game of hanging a maximum number of guns on the B-17s, B-24s and B-25s of the 5th Air Force.

While it can be seen that terrain and climate added to the problems of aircraft maintenance in this direct manner, the indirect effect was infinitely greater. No matter how good the condition of men arriving in the theatre, the combined effects of inadequate diet and the unrelenting need of physical labour for long periods of each day soon had them worn out and vulnerable to disease.

Although high command was fully aware that improved diet would do much to help the situation, large scale supplies of fresh food required nonexistent refrigerated vessels. Transport aircraft would be capable of flying in perishable foods with the necessary speed, but far more vital offensive cargo had first call on their limited capacity, leaving no storage for creature comforts.

The uninteresting canned diet that was available, plus the peculiarities of a tropical climate, meant that most men soon lost 15-20lb (7-9kg) in weight and this, coupled with an 18-hour working day, rapidly reduced their resistance. At Port Moresby the men were plagued by diarrhoea or dysentery, seemingly endemic to the district and everywhere, sooner or later, all fell victim to the malaria-carrying mosquito. They had not then learned the hard truth that protection

Above: Republic P-47 Thunderbolts were valuable escorts for the Liberators striking at distant targets. The earlier models were short on range, and this one just failed to make its base on Noemfoor Island.

Above right: At Eniwetok, Marshall Islands, a Liberator taxies out for take-off to attack the Japanese stronghold at Truk Atoll.

Right: B-24 Liberators over Truk Atoll. The broken line towards the lower edge of the picture is the rim of the coral reef.

against malaria was essential and was necessarily the responsibility of the individual. Slacks and long-sleeved shirts were a first-line of protection. So were mosquito nets but the tropical heat encouraged the men not to use them. Regular dosage of quinine or atabrine was equally essential, but few at first would display the common-sense to take it.

As is common with servicemen the world over, men of the 27th Group learned the hard way, and conditions slowly improved. The number of men reporting sick gradually diminished as they learned to treat the malarial mosquito with respect and as the shipping position improved so did the supply of fresh meat and vegetables. When the military situation began to change for the better, even if then it was merely a case of staying put rather than running away, morale began to improve. In this respect the regular receipt of mail helped considerably and Kenney did all possible to ensure that occasionally, at any rate, men had an opportunity for a brief respite in Australia.

Such organisation helped those in places like Moresby, not far from the Australian mainland, and where a fair sized unit had built up. It was different when men arrived at advanced island bases to discover that maintenance would have to be carried out under the open sky in conditions of heat and humidity, that once again their diet would come solely from cans, and that when near-exhausted they could count themselves fortunate to be able to crawl into leaky tents and try and find some rest.

Far left: Liberators of the 7th Air Force over Truk Atoll, and this unique photograph shows most of this formidable enemy base in the central Pacific.

Left: Dublon Island, within Truk Atoll, receives its fair share of attention from the B-24s.

Below left: Surprisingly, the Japanese did have some humorists. Their greeting was given appropriate quotation marks by air force bomb craters.

Bottom left: Makin Island, in the Gilberts Group, provides a temporary home for this squadron of Douglas A-24s. Slow, short on range and vulnerable to attack, they were not a popular machine.

Right: But these P-39 Airacobras, also seen on Makin, although of much earlier vintage to the A-24s were far superior. Small, fast and manoeuvrable, they remained in the thick of battle until gradually replaced by the more advanced P-38s, P-47s and P-51s.

Below: At Makin too, as on all the other islands stretched across a vast ocean, came the same sad story: the graves of those whose fight for freedom had already ended.

TARAWA ATOLL
HAWKINS FIELD

The problem was made even more difficult by the fact that on most islands the Army and Navy would be working side-by-side. The Navy, which controlled the shipping, provided everything within reason to keep USN personnel in comfort. Morale of Air Force ground crews could hardly be at its best after a month's unchanged diet of Spam, while the adjoining Navy mess hall offered its men fresh meat, vegetables, ice cream, coffee, sugar and refrigerated beer. Neither did a leaking tent pitched on a log floor covered by a tarpaulin compare very favourably with the Navy's quonset huts, built off the ground and equipped with hospital-type spring beds. Inevitably, Army-Navy relations suffered which did little to help the continuation of close and harmonious co-operation.

What of the flying crews? One could argue that their conditions were far worse. Inevitably they suffered the same standards of food and accommodation and were equally prone to the effects of climate and disease; they substituted flying operations for maintenance duties, and few ground crews would have wished to change places with them.

Their prime enemy was a combination of distance and the unfriendly sea. Reconnaissance of or attacks upon islands at the extreme range of their aircraft was the unending nightmare, one in which a change of wind could spell the difference between life and death. Even attacks mounted against enemy-held islands at close range were fraught with hazard, for an aircraft damaged by enemy weapons had little real chance of survival unless it could reach a friendly airfield. Unoccupied islands that might seem to offer some sort of sanctuary were little more than heavily wooded death traps, steaming in moist tropical heat, choked with jungle growth and home only to fever-bearing insects and poisonous reptiles.

It was better to take a chance at ditching, in the hope that the crew could survive long enough in a dinghy to be spotted and rescued.

Left: Once uninhabited islands became unsinkable aircraft carriers in the vastness of the Pacific, such as Hawkins Field, Tarawa Atoll in the Gilberts Group.

Below left: Kwajalein Atoll, in the Marshall Islands Group, was to become the headquarters of the 7th Air Force.

Right: In August of 1944 this wilderness of Guam Island held only a single Japanese airstrip.

Below: One year later it presented a very different picture, having become a major US base.

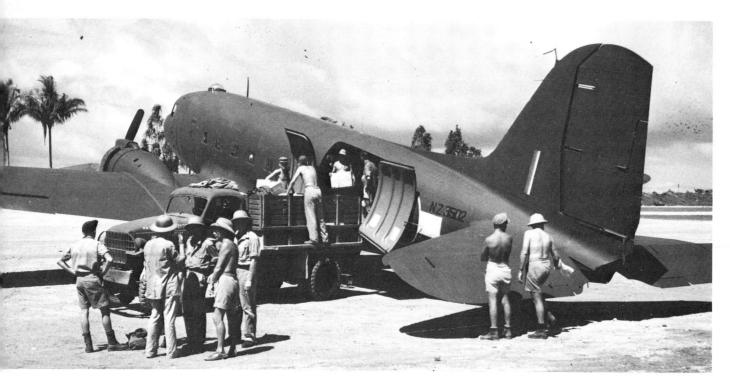

Even this was a pretty forlorn hope in the early days because of an acute shortage of dinghy radio transmitters, without which it was impossible to give some sort of position to would-be air or surface rescuers.

Little wonder that the air crews of the long-range aircraft, constantly airborne because of the limited number of machines available, should suffer extremes of operational fatigue. 'To them there appears no end – just on and on till the Jap gets them', was the comment of the Commanding General South Pacific Area, Gen Harmon.

Distance and unpredictable weather combined to provide the Japanese with another valuable ally. Operations were frequently flown at ranges of up to 2,700 miles (4,345 km), over featureless sea that provided no intermediate landmarks. Accurate navigation was critical to locate a pinpoint target a thousand or more miles away; weather reports, when available, were often unreliable and radio navigation aids were primitive. Even when radio transmitters and receivers worked 100%, intervening tropical storms frequently blanketed reception of life saving information. It is hardly surprising that many aircraft and their crews just disappeared quietly into the infinity of nothingness and were never heard of again.

Time was to bring the solution of most of these problems. More and improved aircraft, reserve flying crews, better standards of maintenance and long-range fighter escort, all contributed to greater reliability and reduced crew fatigue.

One other kind of problem went hand-in-hand as, slowly but surely, the Air Force followed the island road back to Japan.

Above left: Supplies were the ever constant problem. Until the later stages of the war the Navy tended to care for its own. Air force supplies had to come by air, restricting scope and volume. A New Zealand Air Force C-47 being unloaded at Torokina Airstrip, Bougainville.

Left: While combined forces were slowly working their way back across the Japanese-held islands Oahu, Hawaii, which had taken the initial blow, had become a vital training base. It even held such sophistications as this Link trainer, and radio-controlled target aircraft for gunner training, like these Culver PQ-8As (below left), and was amassing aircraft ready for the move into the Marianas. This was *the* vital area, from which the B-29 Superforts would be able to strike at the Japanese homeland.

Above: A line up of P-47 Thunderbolts at Bellows Field, Oahu, in May 1944.

Every new island was covered by dense jungle or coconut groves which had to be hacked away to provide an airstrip, living sites, and areas for stores, fuel and ammunition. Never before had a fighting force advanced over such vast areas in constant conflict with nature as well as a bitterly resistant enemy. It was a rare event to come upon an island with the least vestige of civilised life, living or dead. Practically everything necessary to make it temporarily habitable had to be brought ashore and most of the construction work relied upon laborious hand labour. Only a combination of skill, ingenuity, sweat and sheer guts made such an advance possible. That it left a reserve of will power to eliminate the enemy is little short of miraculous, but serves also as an untarnishable memorial to the Army Air Force.

All of this brought constant and inevitable sapping of the strongest morale. Chaplains and Special Services officers did their utmost to help their men on islands that were isolated by thousands of miles of sea from the nearest areas of conventional civilisation. Recreation centred on the ubiquitous card game, dice, letter-writing and reading and an occasional umpteenth-rate film. Once in a blue moon came the miracle of a live entertainer. Even a mediocre comedienne or female vocalist whose billing before the war would have needed to be read with a magnifying glass could not have received greater acclaim or affection if she had been topping the bill on Broadway.

Unfortunately, improvement in the availability of air transport as the war progressed brought a rift in the brotherhood that mutual suffering and endeavour had once served as a bond between flying and ground crews. Air warfare inevitably reserves the more glamorous role for those who fire the guns or drop the bombs, for it must be accepted that they stand to forfeit their lives on every sortie. To them goes the major share of acclaim for success and by the same token they are first to benefit from improving conditions.

Increased availability of air transport eventually enabled flying crews to be rotated on a fairly regular basis. On average they were flown back to civilisation every three months, spending nine days of leave before returning to the fight. It was necessary and desirable, for long periods of unrelieved operations brought inefficiency in combat and a mounting accident rate.

But for the ground crews the monotonous and exhausting routine went on endlessly, month after month, without hope of relief except for death or the unlikely end of the war. A survey at the beginning of 1944 showed that over 24,000 man days had been lost in the month of December 1943 by 13th Air Force ground personnel who had reported sick.

While high command was fully aware of this unfortunate situation they were helpless to find a remedy. The rift between air and ground crews widened to an extent that never again, during or after the war, did the same feeling of brotherhood return. It is hardly surprising that the airmen who sweated it out on the ground paraphrased the Declaration of Independence to describe their 'superiors', taking from it the words 'All men are created equal', but adding sardonically a dash of Orwell – 'but some are more equal than others'.

6
This and That

Left: As the war continued, new weapons were being readied. This Thunderbolt carries an improvisation: an auxiliary fuel tank converted as a napalm bomb.

In every war, in every age, there are interesting items to record which have little material effect on the outcome of the main engagement but are the gossamer from which legends are spun. Although this book deals with the history of the USAAF in the Pacific, to put things in perspective it is necessary to broaden the picture a little by including brief details of the Battles of the Coral Sea and Midway, primarily US Navy concerns. This chapter serves this purpose and also, in its latter part, rounds off the USAAF participation by including the activities of the 11th Air Force in the north Pacific.

Raid on Tokyo

Typical of the events which have gained a permanent place in Air Force history is the Doolittle raid on Tokyo, made in April 1942, only four months after the Japanese attack on Pearl Harbor.

This brilliantly planned assault on the enemy capital city had originated in the mind of Capt Francis Low of the USN who, as early 10 January 1942, had proposed to a superior officer that he considered it might be possible to convey a small force of Army bombers on board an aircraft carrier to within striking distance of the Japanese home islands. A successful attack against an important target would do much for American morale – then at its lowest ebb – and at the same time would give the Japanese something to think about.

The suggestion was considered worthy of investigation and soon Capt Donald Duncan, USN, had the task of deciding whether the proposition was realistic. After considering the performance of aircraft which might conceivably operate from a carrier, Duncan, who was a Navy pilot, decided that the B-25 Mitchell was the only worthwhile 'possible'. Within days he had presented a detailed plan to Adm Ernest King who, in turn, put the proposition to Gen 'Hap' Arnold. Together they sought and gained approval of the plan from the President and Arnold lost little time in requesting Duncan to supervise initial tests to confirm that a B-25 could get airborne from a carrier deck. Within hours he was able to tell him that a stripped, lightly-loaded B-25 could take off within 500ft (152m). Shortly afterwards a successful take-off was made from a new carrier, the USS Hornet.

Such an orthodox attack needed a leader who could cope with the endless problems that would arise. Arnold selected the master of unorthodoxy, Lt-Col 'Jimmy' Doolittle. A skilled aeronautical engineer, a brilliant pilot and a born leader of men, Doolittle was undoubtedly the right man for the operation. When briefed for the task he confirmed independently that the B-25 Mitchell was the only aircraft capable of doing the job and

satisfied himself that he could pull the Mitchell off the ground in less than 500ft.

No time was lost in preparing for the operation and the 16 B-25s allocated were stripped of their Norden bombsights, ventral gun turrets and W/T radios and their fuel tankage was increased to 1,141 US gallons (4,319 litres). Special equipment included a makeshift bombsight and an auto-pilot for each aircraft, plus two dummy guns mounted in the tail cone to discourage enemy fighters from making an attack from behind.

While Doolittle spent every waking hour in ensuring that no detail was overlooked, pilots drawn from the 17th Bomb Group and 89th Reconnaissance Squadron spent their days in practising how to lift their machines from the ground within the specified distance. In the last days of March all was ready and the sixteen aircraft were loaded aboard the USS Hornet at San Francisco. On 1 April, less than three months from the birth of Low's idea, the Hornet put to sea.

The plan of attack required the Hornet, outwardly an ordinary carrier within a normal task force, to approach within 400 miles (644km) of the Japanese coastline. At that distance the B-25s would have sufficient endurance to find their targets and fly on to landing grounds in China where, having refuelled, they would rendezvous at Chunking. The risk of the carrier being intercepted at a range greater than 400 miles had to be accepted. The possibility of a chance meeting with enemy air or naval patrols up to 1,500 miles (2,414km) from the target could have involved committing the aircraft and their crews to a one-way mission with little hope of survival. When Doolittle briefed his crews to this effect on board the Hornet, every man was quite prepared to accept the chances.

Left: First significant air strike made on the enemy was that of Doolittle's raiders, who attacked Tokyo from the carrier USS Hornet on 18 April 1942. Here the North American B-25 Mitchells are being prepared for the attack.

Above: Jimmy Doolittle and his crew, together with some Chinese helpers, photographed after they had baled out of their aircraft over China, following the attack on Tokyo.

At 0630hrs on 18 April, when the *Hornet* was still some 800 miles (1,287km) from the Japanese coast, an enemy patrol vessel came within visual contact. Although the cruiser *Northampton* was despatched immediately to destroy her there could be little doubt that Japanese naval intelligence would have been advised of the position of the American task force. The moment for take off had come.

None of Doolittle's crews had even seen a Mitchell take off from a carrier. It was up to 'Jimmy' to show that it could be done. With flaps down and engines at full power he pulled off the deck with a 100ft (30m) to spare. One by one the remainder followed and soon all were headed at low level over the angry seas of the Pacific towards their target – Tokyo.

They reached the Japanese coast without meeting any opposition, maintaining treetop height over the land until Tokyo was sighted and then climbed steeply to their attack level of 1,500ft (457m). Surprise was complete and the enemy put up little opposition as the Mitchells roared over the capital, dropping their bombs on their assigned targets. It seemed little more than seconds before it was all over. The rest it seemed would be easy for the force was to be 'homed' by radio to their destination in China and guided finally by landing flares. But however good the intentions, there was no guidance of any

Above left: From the Gilberts to the Marshalls was the next north-west move. Typical of the pre-invasion treatment that could then be dished out is seen at Jaluit Island, a Japanese seaplane and submarine base.

Above: Returning from a strike against the Marshalls, a Liberator makes a one-wheel landing as ambulance and fire tenders stand by.

Below: Rocket-propelled weapons came into more general use as the war advanced. This Douglas A-20, better known to the British as the Boston, is being fitted with rocket-launcher tubes.

Above: A reconnaissance photograph of Tokyo, the blackened areas representing those burned out in a daylight incendiary attack on 25 February 1945.

Above right: The Japanese did not limit themselves to fighter defence. Retaliatory strikes were made against the Marianas bases, and this attack on Iseley Field completely destroyed three Superforts and caused considerable damage to other parked aircraft.

Right: But even at this later stage of the war wrecked aircraft still had great value. This skeleton of a B-29 is being systematically stripped of all reusable components.

kind. As the Mitchells combed the unfamiliar Chinese countryside seeking a haven, engines coughed to a standstill as tanks ran dry. The majority of the crews had no alternative but to bale out or 'ditch' just off the coast. Remarkably all but four of the crews survived, though many had to face years of imprisonment.

What had been gained? When Doolittle considered this question on the following day he felt that 16 aircraft had been thrown away for very little. He was not to know, until very much later, that although damage to enemy installations was insignificant, these 16 courageous crews had achieved a great deal. Their action was almost certainly responsible for the retention in Japan of four fighter groups which the enemy needed urgently in the south Pacific. More important, the Japanese over-extended themselves in a desperate attempt to prevent a repetition of the attack. The biggest gain was psychological: spelling uncertainly to the enemy and heartening the American nation with the knowledge that its armed forces could, and would, hit back at the Japanese homeland.

Battle of Midway

As we have seen earlier, 5th Air Force B-17s were faced daily with the unenviable and monotonous task of reconnaissance over endless miles of open sea. Day after day there was nothing to relieve the sapping combination of boredom and tension, but during April 1942 they were able to alert American intelligence to the fact that Japanese forces were concentrating at Rabaul and that a move to capture Port Moresby seemed imminent. Immediately, Adm Chester W. Nimitz, Commander-in-Chief, Pacific Fleet, assembled in the Coral Sea all available naval forces.

By 1 May this comprised the carriers USS *Lexington* and *Yorktown*, supported by five cruisers, and three days later they were reinforced by a sixth American cruiser and two from the Royal Australian Navy.

Because of heavy losses of aircraft in an attempt to invade Ceylon at the beginning of April, three Japanese carriers had been compelled to return to the homeland to refit. Thus, the task force for the attack on Port Moresby was limited to only two carriers, the *Zuikaku* and *Shokaku*, supported by two cruisers and six destroyers.

In the first days of May these two forces played a grim game of hide-and-seek until, on 7 May, aircraft from the *Yorktown* reported contact with two enemy carriers and four cruisers. Rear-Adm Fletcher, commanding *Yorktown*, believed this to be the enemy striking force but, in fact, it was a weaker group escorting the invasion transports, which included the light carrier *Shoho*. All available American aircraft were flown off to attack this force. The *Shoho* was soon destroyed and the transports, deprived of air support, withdrew hastily. But this action had revealed to both sides the positions of the main task forces. At about 1100hrs on 8 May, the carrier-borne aircraft of each force struck almost simultaneously. The *Shokaku* was damaged severely, but managed to limp home, the *Zuikaku* was undamaged. On the American side the *Yorktown* received slight damage but the *Lexington* was hit hard and was soon ablaze. Despite heroic attempts to salvage her, she was devastated by an internal explosion and an uncontrollable fire resulted in her being abandoned. The *coup de grace* came from an American torpedo.

Although the honours were slightly in favour of the Japanese, naval historians rank

Left: The P-47 Thunderbolt was an invaluable weapon, neutralising pockets of Japanese on nearby islands within the Marianas group, flying escort missions (below) even if delivery of pilots to the dispersal points was a little archaic (top right). But there was nothing primitive about their weapons, their eight 0.5in machine guns supplemented by rockets (centre right), and they lost little time in 'rocketing' off the ground when called upon for a strike (bottom right).

this an important air/sea confrontation in the Pacific and a psychological victory for the Americans. It was the first naval engagement in history in which the opposing vessels had not fired a single shot at each other. The USN had discovered, as had Doolittle's tiny force, that the enemy was not invincible and took new heart. Furthermore, the invasion force menacing Port Moresby had been forced to withdraw.

To the Japanese it posed a serious problem, for their continued domination of the newly-won territories depended upon retaining their control over the freedom of the seas. Admiral Yamamoto was determined that the American fleet must be brought to battle and destroyed. Accordingly, he planned to seize Midway Island and simultaneously, to attack the western Aleutians. By careful timing he hoped to lure the American fleet from the area of Midway, seize the island and be prepared for the inevitable immediate naval counter-attack. With superior strength, particularly in fast battleships, he felt confident that he could eliminate the American fleet once and for all.

Once again, USAAF reconnaissance aircraft enabled Adm Nimitz to have a pretty shrewd idea of the enemy's plan and he gathered his forces for the clash. He also had an ace up his sleeve, being able to count on powerful air support from the 7th Air Force squadrons based on Midway. It was they who, on 4 June, first pinpointed the position of the Japanese aircraft carriers.

Without delaying a moment, the Americans launched the attack, torpedo bombers from the USS *Enterprise*, *Hornet* and *Yorktown* seeking to get in the first telling blow. In this they were unsuccessful, for the enemy's defence was too strong. But, while the Japanese interceptors were concentrating on their task of destroying the torpedo bombers, a force of 37 dive bombers from the *Enterprise* and *Yorktown* were able to sneak in, almost unopposed, to launch their attack on the carriers *Akagi* and *Kaga*. Almost simultaneously, 17 aircraft from the *Yorktown* struck at the carrier *Soryu*. Within minutes all three ships were ablaze from stem to stern; devastating fires raged below decks and it was clear they were doomed.

Enemy reaction was fast and furious and despite the most spirited defence *Yorktown* was soon damaged severely. Courageous efforts got the resulting fires under control and she was taken in tow, clear of the action: two days later she was sunk by an enemy submarine.

But long before the *Yorktown* was sunk, the fourth and last of Yamamoto's carriers, the *Hiryu*, had settled into the Pacific deeps, torn into a flaming wreck by aircraft flown off the *Enterprise*. Immediately the remainder of the enemy fleet was ordered to withdraw, for without protection of an air umbrella they too would soon join the tangled wreckage in the ocean depths.

It was disaster for Yamamoto, for the loss of the carriers meant that the spearhead of his naval striking force was broken: to add to the bitterness of the defeat, he had lost over 200 irreplaceable naval pilots, the most experienced of the men who had fought their way across the Pacific.

The Battle of Midway marked a turning point in the Pacific War: without domination of the sea lanes it was inevitable that the Japanese should be forced on to the defensive. There was worse to come: soon they were to lose the man who had master-minded the navy's strategy, Adm Isoroku Yamamoto.

Intercepting Yamamoto

On 18 April, 1943, exactly 12 months after the Doolittle raid on Tokyo, 16 P-38s of the 13th Air Force's 112th, 70th and 339th Fighter Squadrons intercepted and destroyed over the island of Bougainville in the Solomons a Japanese bomber. It carried as a passenger Adm Yamamoto.

This was no chance encounter, for five days earlier one of the hundreds of the Japanese radio transmissions, which were monitored as routine, was seen when decoded to have an unusually large number of addressees, suggesting that it might have more than average importance. It was passed to a senior officer of the translation department, who polished the original still further, to discover that it had been originated by the commander of the Japanese 8th Fleet. It proved to be an inspection itinerary for the Imperial Japanese Navy's commander-in-chief, detailed to the minute and there wasn't an officer in the US forces who didn't know that this commander was the father of the 'infamy': Adm Yamamoto.

On the following morning the decoded message lay on the desk of Adm Nimitz. It needed little discussion between Nimitz and his senior intelligence officer to decide that an attempt should be made to intercept and destroy Yamamoto's transport. As a national hero and the Japanese Navy's bold strategist, his death would be a major psychological victory. With little time to mount the attack, a message was sent to Adm Halsey's executive officer. By the following morning, 15 April, the operation was approved.

Messages flurried around the chain of command, one reaching Rear-Adm Marc Mitscher on Guadalcanal, upon whom responsibility for organising the operation was to rest. To his office reported Maj John Mitchell and Capt Thomas G. Lanphier of the USAAF, summoned to plan and lead this important mission. As finalised, Mitchell would have overall command; Lanphier would lead a first 'killer' section of four P-38s. In all, the pilots of 18 aircraft were briefed for the operation: eight each from the 12th and 339th Squadrons, two from the 70th.

To provide the necessary range for the P-38G Lightnings, 5th Air Force B-24s from Moresby ferried in new large drop tanks, and squadron fitters worked through the night to fabricate special shackles and attach them to the fighters.

Finally came the vitally important briefing, emphasising the points that time and position of interception must be precisely as instructed, and that 435-mile (700km) outward flight must follow a circuitous wave-top-height course to avoid detection.

At 0725hrs on 18 April 1943, the P-38s began their take-off from Henderson Field. One veered off the airstrip, almost out of control as a loose matting spike ripped away a main wheel tyre: minutes after take-off another had to abort when its pilot discovered there was no petrol feed from the new drop tanks.

The remaining aircraft roared towards Bougainville, barely cresting the Pacific swell. One came so low that a propellor 'caught a crab', blinding the canopy with spray so that, for a split second, it seemed it must plunge to destruction on the unyielding water. Happily it survived. Sixteen P-38s were speeding towards their rendezvous with two Mitsubishi G4M1 bombers (Bettys) of the Japanese 705th Bombardment Squadron, escorted by six Mitsubishi A6M Zeros (Zekes) of the 309th Fighter Squadron.

At 0934hrs, one minute before the scheduled interception time, a pilot of one of the covering groups of P-38s spotted the enemy exactly where expected. It was almost as if the meeting had been prearranged on both sides. Recognition must have been simultaneous, for the two Bettys turned away as the Zeros came streaking in to try and prevent an attack. They were outnumbered and within minutes it was all over. One Betty, subsequently found to be the one carrying the Navy's commander-in-chief, careened in flame amidst Bougainville's jungle: the other crashed into the sea. Yamamoto was dead.

The psychological effect of this action cannot be measured. That it shook the Japanese nation to the core is certain and had they known it was a deliberately meditated action their reaction might have been savage, resulting in even more violent treatment of Allied prisoners. Fortunately they did not know this, believing it to be a haphazard interception by a routine patrol. They imagined that their message codes, complex multi-digit basic groups with mis-leading additives, were impregnable. Years after came the Japanese comment that the Yamamoto tragedy had seemed almost prophetic: '. . . after his death came no more major victories, only steadily increasing disasters'.

Balloon Bombing

However, the Americans did not hold a monopoly on the unusual. One of their vesssels on a routine patrol off the Californian coast on 4 November 1944, spotted floating on the surface of the sea what appeared to be a large piece of cloth. It was of sufficient interest to warrant a close look and accordingly the order to change course was given. When the vessel drew alongside and the 'cloth' was hauled on board it was found to be a rubberised silk balloon to which was attached a strange metallic device and a small radio transmitter of Japanese origin.

Not surprisingly it caused something of a stir, and when a second example was recovered from the sea a little later and, subsequently, other examples were found on the American mainland, it became clear to US intelligence officers that the Japanese were deploying some kind of airborne weapon against the American continent.

As extensive searches began to turn up other examples, some with high explosive and incendiary weapons attached, it was realised that here was a potentially dangerous weapon that if deployed on a large scale could cause considerable physical damage. There was also the psychological effect of such a weapon to consider for if the American public were to realise that a sinister, silent and possibly deadly weapon might be drifting down on them at any time in large numbers, there would be real and considerable alarm.

After careful consideration it was agreed that the best defence was to keep the information as secret as possible. Then not only would the American public be unaware that the enemy was launching a most unorthodox attack against continental America but also, if strict censorship prevented the Japanese from discovering the success of these operations, they might be discouraged from continuing to deploy the weapon.

This was the action taken and it proved to be the right method of dealing with the situation. Believing that their very considerable efforts were not achieving success, the Japanese decided that the manpower and productive effort involved was not worthwhile and after some months of these operations brought the launchings to a halt.

Consequently, few Americans were aware of these weapons and no information was released until late May 1945 when, following the death of six people near Lakeview,

Oregon it was decided to warn the public against touching any balloon-like object they might discover. By then the war against Japan was mounting in intensity and the enemy was fully occupied in dealing with devastating attacks being made upon his home islands by American air power.

What then was the origin and form of this highly ingenious weapon that was, in fact, being launched not far distant from Tokyo itself? For details we are indebted to the extensive and carefully documented research of Mr Robert C. Mikesh, a curatorial assistant of the Aeronautics department of the Smithsonian Institution, Washington, DC.

Following early research in America, Mr Mikesh had the opportunity of investigating the matter in detail during a considerable period of time that he spent in Japan. He was able to examine original documents and talk with Japanese officers who had been involved in the project.

The idea had originated in the early 1930s, but it was not until the Pacific War was well advanced that the scheme was reconsidered and developed into an operational weapon. Meterological studies had shown that high altitude air streams which attained a maximum velocity over Japan in the period between November and March should be capable of carrying a balloon from Japan across the Pacific to and over the American continent. Launch of small balloons carrying radiosonde equipment confirmed that the idea was feasible. Efforts were then concentrated on perfecting a device that would enable a balloon to maintain a predetermined altitude and, at the appropriate time after launch, release its offensive weapon.

Having calculated that the transoceanic crossing would take two or three days the Japanese scientists and engineers had to evolve some method that would allow a hydrogen filled balloon to maintain its desired altitude despite the fact that high day and low night temperatures would cause very considerable changes in lift. The high temperature, without any form of control, would allow the balloon to gain altitude when it would eventually burst. The converse applied at night, when low temperature would cause loss of buoyancy and altitude.

The controlling device in its finalised form relied upon a barometric control to switch current to explosive fittings from which were hung bags of ballast, and high explosive or incendiary bombs. This control worked in conjunction with a pressure relief valve on the balloon envelope. If under high temperature conditions the balloon rose to an altitude where pressure within the envelope was too high, the pre-set relief valve would vent hydrogen, reducing lift and stabilising the balloon's level. If reduced temperature or gas loss caused the balloon to fall below the predetermined height for which the aneroid of the barometric control was set, current would be switched to fire an explosive cartridge to release a pair of bags containing ballast. In this manner the balloon could be maintained within certain height levels, usually between 37,000 and 30,000ft (11,280 and 9,145m), in which altitude band the high speed air streams were blowing eastward towards the United States.

Calculations had estimated the theoretical number of rise and fall cycles the balloon would make during its transoceanic crossing. A final signal for the release of ballast would, instead, drop offensive weapons, hopefully over the target area.

The unorthodox weapon worked and Mr Mikesh has recorded the recovery or identification of 285 of these balloons on or near to the land mass of America and Canada. He has also been able to establish that approximately 9,000 of them were launched in the period November 1944 to early April 1945. Thus, in respect of finding the target, there was a success rate of something over 3%. This may not seem very good economics but one must appreciate that even if this small number of weapons had hit and set fire to a major factory, or destroyed by fire a significant area of one of the west coast timber regions, it would have been well worthwhile.

There seems little doubt that if the Japanese had been aware that 3% of their balloons were homing successfully on the transPacific target, then considerably more effort would have been put into the operation. And it is not unreasonable to suppose that with continued success it would have evolved as a far more deadly weapon. They could, just as easily, have carried to the American continent the more poisonous fruits of chemical and biological warfare.

Mining Operations

At a later stage of the war the USAAF was to deploy against Japan what was, for the air force, an unusual airborne weapon, and this is as good a place as any to take a look at these operations.

When Japan entered the war she had a sizable fleet of shipping estimated at around six million tons to which was added nearly another million tons acquired in her early conquests. But with large garrisons of men to maintain on very distant islands and outposts its total was really inadequate and the inroads of Allied submarine and air activity was causing wastage well beyond the replacement capability of Japan's shipbuilding industry. So serious was the situation towards the end of 1944 that she was forced to abandon regular contact with the remnants

Left: Angaur Island in the Carolines Group offered a valuable base for support to the Marianas, as well as a stepping stone to the Philippines. Runway under construction on 22 October 1944.

Below: Four days later the Liberators had arrived, while work groups were still busy consolidating hard standings.

Below, centre: By December it was a major base, fully operational as shown in this air photograph.

Bottom: Crews being briefed in the open at Angaur for a strike against Araka Besan, Palu Islands, a stage nearer to the Philippines.

of units still offering resistance to the Allies at peripheral bases.

The mountainous and island nature of the Japanese homeland had limited road and rail communications, consequently shipping lanes within the Inland Sea had always been of great importance, When the Americans occupied Iwo Jima, the southern exit from this sea became hazardous. This left only the Shimonoseki Strait, between Honshu and Kyushu, as a comparatively safe exit to the Pacific, without a lengthy time-and-fuel-consuming trip to the north of Honshu.

With invasion of Okinawa imminent, the US Navy were anxious to limit the activity of Japanese sea power and pressed the USAAF to undertake mining activities with the primary objective of limiting or preventing use of the Shimonoseki Strait. This came at the time when the USAAF was first beginning to build up its strength of Boeing B-29 Superfortresses and when the minds of USAAF planners were full of ideas of launching massive attacks against the home islands of Japan.

Gen Arnold and his staff were not very enthusiastic at Navy intervention in their plans. At long last on the brink of making telling strikes against the sources of enemy production, they were loath to dilute the strength of their then somewhat limited efforts at strategic bombing by diverting aircraft in direct support of the Navy. When their studies showed that mining of the narrow channel between Honshu and Kyushu would be of significance to the common cause, however, they gave the fullest co-operation possible.

It was no simple task, for it required modifications to the B-29s involved in carrying the parachute mines. Furthermore, with no real knowledge of this particular type of weapon, both air and ground crews had to assimilate a lot of instruction provided by

Above: In early raids on the enemy home islands from the Marianas, the long range involved a careful balance of fuel and bomb load. A sudden wind shift could make all the difference and this Superfort didn't quite make its Saipan base.

the Navy. Further problems came from a difficult supply situation, leaving little time to modify, load and arm the mines for different types of mission.

The need for accurate placing of the mines was clear and this meant that high altitude daylight attacks were out. Since the mines were carried to the surface by parachute the lower the altitude from which they were dropped, the better the chance of them arriving where intended. This restricted operations to comparatively low-level attacks by night but fortunately the B-29s were equipped with radar which would simplify the problem of dropping the weapon in the right place.

The first attack was made on the Shimonoseki Strait on the night of 27/28 March 1945, when 105 B-29s took-off, each carrying a 12,000lb (5,445kg) load of 1,000lb and 2,000lb acoustic and magnetic mines. Flying at altitudes varying from 5,000 to 8,000ft (1,525-2,440m) 92 of the bombers covered the primary target area. A second mission flown on the night of 30/31 March added to the coverage and, in addition, made sure that the approaches to Sasebo, Kure and Horishima had their share of these underwater hazards.

The Japanese were not slow in reacting to these attacks. Soon well over 300 vessels and some 20,000 men were involved in trying to sweep clear routes for their shipping. They were not completely unsuccessful but coped fairly well with the acoustic mines. The magnetic mines posed more of a problem and the pressure mines proved too much for them.

Mine-laying operations extended over a period of 4½ months, during which period more than 12,000 mines were sown in Japan's home waters. This was a far greater effort than had been aticipated by the USAAF at the outset and was accomplished for the loss of only 16 aircraft. Had it been worthwhile?

Following the early attacks, Japanese shipping refused to move at all until a clear

channel had been swept. But, simultaneously with these mining operations, the B-29s were introducing the Japanese to ordeal by fire. Food stocks became so short that shipping had to keep moving, regardless of the risk, and losses began to build up. Suffice it to say that during the single month of June 1945 Japanese shipping losses totalled some 311,000 tons, attributed as follows: submarines 95,000 tons; aircraft attack 56,000 tons; USAAF minelaying operations 163,000 tons, more than half of this latter figure in the Shimonoseki Strait. In its final postwar assessment of the figures, mining activities (largely by the B-29s) were accredited with over 800,000 tons of enemy shipping destroyed.

The Aleutians

It has been mentioned earlier that many of the USAAF squadrons based on very far-flung and, until the Pacific War, uninhabited islands, regarded themselves as forgotten. If any of the US Army Air Forces merited such a claim, there seems little doubt that the 11th Air Force had the most justification. Their war was perhaps the most frustrating of all, fought, in the main, against appalling weather rather than the enemy.

In the north Pacific, stretching out from Alaska like a broken string of beads, are the Aleutian Islands. The most remote, Attu, lies more than a 1,000 miles (1,610km) from the last unbroken segment of the Alaskan Peninsular. So far across the Pacific do the beads stretch, that Attu is only about 400 miles (645km) from Russia's Far East province of Kamchatka.

In 1942 this chain of islands, with the exception of Unalaska, were uninhabited and unfortified. On 3 June 1942, under cover of a diversionary attack against Dutch Harbor, spearheaded by carrier-based aircraft from the *Ryujo* and *Junyo*, the Japanese occupied the most westerly islands of Attu, Agattu and Kiska. This was a purely defensive move, intended to prevent any American advance on Japan via the Aleutians.

It was a wise and realistic move on the part of the Japanese, for despite the inhospitable nature of these volcanic islands, bounded on their northern side by the Bering Sea and icebound from October to April, they were nevertheless considered by some planners to offer one route to Tokyo. Those particular planners were, however, of the chairborne variety, with no first hand knowledge of the terrain and of these bleak and windswept islands which, for much of the year, play hide-and-seek in an environment of fog.

This was the theatre of operations for the 11th Air Force and one in which, despite determined efforts, was by virtue of the weather, to remain one of the most inactive throughout the remainder of the war. One isolated statistic will pinpoint the problem: so difficult was (and is) the weather that the Japanese-held islands at the western end of the chain rarely had more than 10 clear days in a year!

As a result, the long-range attacks by B-17s and B-24s against the enemy were, in the main confined to dropping bombs through holes in the overcast. By the time they hit, or missed, their targets the cloud pattern had changed and visual confirmation of success or failure was impossible. It was not long before this routine of bombing through the overcast was discontinued, for it was realised that the cost of the operation in bomb expenditure alone was virtually worthless. As an alternative, it was decided to give the Japanese garrisons the joys of a naval bombardment. Between 22 July and 7 August, aided by reconnaissance and air cover provided by units of the 'Eleventh', the Navy did its best to overcome the weather problem – and failed..

It was then clear that the only solution would be to make landings and eliminate the enemy from their bases. One of the first requirements was an advance base from which aircraft of the 'Eleventh' could operate against the Japanese forces. This needed to be close enough so that the units based there could react quickly to favourable weather reports and strike before the situation had reverted once again to its normal condition of nil visibility.

Adak Island was chosen finally, and on 30 August landings were made, carrying ashore the essential engineers and construction equipment to create an airstrip. No prior survey of the island had been made and the engineers were to discover there was no suitable site to create a conventional airstrip. The unconventional would have to suffice instead.

Accordingly, they selected the only worthwhile level area, a tidal basin, and by dint of great ingenuity and hard work diverted the course of a creek and created a drainage system that kept out both tide and creek water. By mid-September, when the creek bed had been levelled and steel matting laid, the 'Eleventh' had its advanced base, only 250 miles (402km) from the enemy.

The Adak strip proved to be effective and within a short time both fighters and medium bombers were able to begin the reduction of enemy installations and aircraft. Even so, the weather continued to be the most potent adversary for both sides. Of 72 US aircraft lost during one period, only nine were the result of enemy action. It is not surprising that one pilot wrote to a colleague saying: '... Since I arrived the target hasn't been visible. The weather is getting worse. The thing we can't understand is why we continue to send our men out into this god awful stuff against a target which can't be seen nine-tenths of the time and if hit isn't worth the gas burned up to get it ...'

Leapfrogging a little further west, a landing was made on Amchitka Island in mid-January where, by 16 February, another advanced airstrip was in operation. From there fighter-bombers supplemented by bombers operating from Adak were able to maintain regular attacks on the enemy, and it was clear that his days in the Aleutians were numbered. When, on 26 March, the Navy foiled a Japanese task force attempting to replenish the garrisons on Kiska and Attu, the beginning of the end was in sight. Realising that they would soon have a fight on their hands, the enemy withdrew their forces from Agattu to reinforce the positions on Attu.

In preparation for invasion of Attu, air operations were stepped up to a maximum. When, on 11 May initial landings began, it was believed that they would encounter little resistance from the Japanese. Once again, grim weather proved a valuable ally to the enemy, frustrating the main attempts to provide air support in sufficient strength to blunt his counter-attacks. The inevitable result was a protracted and bloody struggle that lasted until the end of the month.

It remained, then, to clear the island of Kiska, involving a much larger landing to eliminate the estimated 8,000 defenders. In preparation, the 'Eleventh' was reinforced, and its Troop Carrier Squadrons brought in large numbers of men and thousands of tons of supplies. Pre-invasion bombardment of Kiska by the battleships *Idaho, Mississippi, New Mexico, Pennsylvania* and *Tennessee* must surely have shattered the enemy positions, already battered by aircraft of the 'Eleventh' on every possible occasion. It was reasonable to assume that the landings might not prove too costly.

On 15 August the first troops went ashore – to anticlimax. Not a single Japanese remained on the island. Under cover of the persistent fog all had been evacuated and the Aleutian campaign was at an end.

Despite the enormous difficulties of these blind-man's buff operations, the US had achieved a worthwhile victory in the north Pacific. The initiative had moved from Japanese to American hands which meant that from the Autumn of 1943 the enemy was forced to maintain large numbers of desperately needed men and aircraft on Hokkaido and the Kuril Islands, to meet any attempted invasion by the Americans from their Aleutian bases. In this respect, if no other, the 11th Air Force could claim to have made a significant contribution to final victory.

7
The Very Long Range Bomber

Left: Last minute checks even include a little spit and polish for, appropriately named, *Special Delivery*.

103

Fulfilment of the promise of air power required the use of long range aircraft to strike at an enemy's industrial productive capacity. The British Air Staff had forseen such a requirement in 1936 and this appreciation led to development of the four-engined Short Stirling, Handley Page Halifax and, via the twin-engined Avro Manchester, the famous Lancaster. These were the aircraft that by night, working in conjunction with the USAAF's B-17 daylight attacks, maintained a round-the-clock battering of German industry.

USAAC planners had been no less far-sighted, hence the B-17 and B-24, but had failed to achieve their requirement for a strategic bomber capable of the range needed to make it suitable for deployment in the Pacific. Gen Benjamin D. Foulois, Chief of the Air Corps from 1931 to 1935, had been a protagonist of the strategic bombardment force. He encouraged sponsorship of the design competition in 1934 which sired Boeing's Model 299, a military development of their Model 300 four-engined civil transport.

The Army's specification had called for a multi-engined bomber with a range of 1,020 to 2,200 miles (1,641 to 3,540km), maximum speed between 200 and 250mph (321 and 402km/h) and capable of lifting a 2,000lb (907kg) bomb load over the specified range. This evolved eventually as the B-17 Flying Fortress and the service test YB-17s (later Y1B-17) with four 930hp Wright GR-1820-

Right: The most successful of the USAAF's fighter pilots was America's 'Ace of aces', Richard I. Bong, who accrued a total of 40 enemy aircraft destroyed by the war's end.

Below: The honour of being the first USAAF aircraft to land on Saipan fell to this Piper L-4 Grasshopper, a military version of the famous Cub. It landed, under fire from the enemy, on 23 June 1944.

Far right, top: By the following day the might of the air force had begun to move in. First came the fighters, followed by hosts of transports similar to these Curtiss C-46s seen at Aslito airstrip.

Far right, bottom: The transports that brought in the urgently needed supplies were, in the early days, assured of a return cargo. Casualties being loaded aboard a C-46 at Saipan.

39 radial engines demonstrated a range, speed and weapon capacity well within the specification requirements. Unfortunately, the Army-Navy controversy over defence responsibility delayed procurement plans and it was not until 1941 that B-17s began to come off the production line in significant numbers.

But long before the B-17 materialised, the Air Corps had initiated specifications for more advanced bombers to satisfy the strategic role. In 1935 Boeing began work on a 5,000 mile (8,045km) range machine which was known originally as Project A and subsequently as the Experimental Bomber Long Range 1 (XBLR-1) later designated XB-15. Similarly, the Douglas Aircraft Company recieved a contract for a competitive XBLR-2 with a maximum bomb load of 37,100lb (16,828kg) and range of 7,710 miles (12,408km). This was later designated XB-19. Although prototypes of both aircraft flew, the power of engines then available was inadequate and both projects were put 'on the shelf'.

With the advent of the Pacific war the need for Very Long Range (VLR) strategic bombers was apparent. Before Pearl Harbor USAAF planners had referred frequently to VHBs (Very Heavy Bombers) but the distances involved in the Pacific theatre were so great that emphasis on range was of greater significance than bomb load and the term VLR bomber became more aptly and generally used. But even before the Japanese attack, Gen Arnold had taxed the War Department to begin development of a VLR bomber, superior in every respect to the B-17 and B-24.

On 29 January 1940, requests for proposals were submitted to five national aircraft manufacturers and the submissions of Boeing, Lockheed, Douglas and Consolidated were allocated the provisional designations XB-29, XB-30, XB-31 and XB-32 respectively. Eventually, Lockheed and Douglas withdrew and on 6 September 1940, contracts were placed with Boeing and Consolidated for the construction of two (later changed to three) prototypes of their respective designs.

First to fly was Consolidated's (Convair's) XB-32 Dominator, on 7 September 1942, but continual requests for changes in its design delayed introduction into service to such an extent that it was not until the closing stages of the war that the 386th Bombardment Squadron with a strength of 15 B-32s, mounted token operations against the Japanese from Yontan airstrip, on Okinawa.

Boeing's XB-29, on the other hand, made far more significant progress and, with a

Above: One of the first B-24s on Saipan was *Bolivar Jr,* taxiing in under the eyes of Maj-Gen Robert W. Douglass (right) and Col Lawrence J. Carr.

Right: Isley Field, Saipan, soon had a healthy population of Liberators (above), as did Agana Field on Guam (below).

growing likelihood of participation in the European conflict, well over 1,5000 had been ordered before the prototype made its first flight on 21 September 1942. The second prototype, which first flew on 28 December 1942, caught fire and crashed tragically on 18 February 1943, killing ten of Boeing's most experienced engineers allocated to the programme. Modifications to reduce the fire hazard caused a delay of several months but in mid-1943 the first pre-production aircraft was handed over to the USAAF for armament and flight testing. And due to the unusual procurement programme, the first production aircraft came off the line in the following month.

It had been a most peculiar gamble for the normally slow-moving procurement department of the Air Force; for the B-29 Superfortress, as it became known, was then a very advanced aeroplane with two pressurised sections in the fuselage, and periscopically-sighted remotely-controlled power-operated gun turrets. Even the initial production version had a maximum speed of 358mph (576km/h), range of 3,250 miles (5,230km), was armed with up to 11 0.50in machine guns and could carry a 20,000lb (9,072kg) bomb load.

Inevitably came the argument as to who should have first call on this important weapon that could, clearly, make a significant contribution in any of the theatres of war. The cardinal point of Anglo-American strategy was a mutual agreement to concentrate on the elimination of Germany before turning to the Pacific theatre where, during the interim period, a purely defensive and holding war was being fought.

If proof were needed of the adherence to this policy, one has only to recall the transfer to the Middle East of General Brereton from the CBI theatre, together with all available bomber and transport aircraft, despite a critical Burma/India situation at that period. With similar determination to snuff out the European/Middle East Conflicts, US Air Staff planners assigned the future B-29s and B-32s a priority role in these latter theatres.

This plan remained virtually unchanged until early 1943, when improving fortune in the Far East suggested that the VLR bombers, intended originally for operations in that theatre, might now be deployed there to very considerable advantage. Even then the issue was far from clear cut, especially when the US Navy wanted an allocation of Superfortresses to maintain a long-range watch on submarines. This was one request that was met with the ungilded comment that the Air Force were not even prepared to discuss it! It was not quite so easy, however, to dismiss valid requests for the use of B-29s in the battles being fought in the CBI area

Top left: It was not long before the 'big boys', the B-29s began to fly in to Saipan.

Above left: Preparations had already been made for their reception, even to the extent of engine changes if necessary, but 'workshops' were still rather primitive.

Left: Nothing could have been more gratifying than the chance, at last, to hit right at the enemy's vitals. Individual souvenirs are prepared for the first Tokyo raid.

Above: Armourers busy themselves loading a percentage of the force with M-69 incendiary clusters.

and in operations mounted from Hawaii, the South Pacific and the Aleutians: in those areas they would prove an invaluable reinforcement.

Circumstances were to decide that their initial operational deployment should be in the Pacific but delineation of inter-service, international and political niceties was to take nearly as much time as had been involved in building the first machines.

Most difficult of the Far East problems was that which existed in the CBI theatre where the Japanese were expanding and consolidating their hold on China and advancing steadily in Burma. This deteriorating situation was causing political complications with the government of General Chiang Kai-shek. It was essential to limit Japanese activities and interminable discussions ended with an agreement to use the B-29s initially to hit at strategic targets in the Japanese home islands operating from advanced bases in China or Formosa.

Estimates that some 300 B-29s should be available by late-1944 and a similar number by the early summer of 1945, offered the potential of a vital striking force. But utilisation of

such a vast force from advanced bases in China posed the nightmare problem of logistic supply over the Hump. Nevertheless, plans were made to construct a string of airfields in China so that they would be sited within a radius of 1,500 miles (2,415km) of major Japanese industrial targets. What were these vital targets?

A committee of Operational Analysts listed the six most vital, not necessarily in this order, as shipping, steel production, the electronic, aircraft and ball-bearing industries, and urban industrial areas. In the final analysis, steel production was placed at the head of the list and, fortuitously, the coke ovens that were the heart of steel production were within range of advanced Chinese bases.

This would seem to have settled the decision, but the increasing successs of combined operations, emanating originally from the South Pacific, gave hope that possible bases in the Mariana group of islands would be of even greater value and far less vulnerable to the Japanese than advanced bases in China. Compromise was the eventual agreement, with initial operations from China, during which valuable experience would be

Below: The great moment at last, as the might of XXIst Bomber Command queues up for take-off and the first of them lifts off Iseley Field for the initial attack on Tokyo, (far left).

Left: The initial raids had only limited success, the high altitude daylight attacks posing many problems. Not surprisingly, the enemy did his best to oppose the attackers, and here a Japanese fighter ('Nick') takes evasive action after a head-on attack.

Above: The need for an intermediate airstrip where aircraft returning from attacks on Japan could put down in emergency speeded plans to invade Iwo Jima. Liberators en route to begin the softening-up process.

Above right: By then, the superb North American P-51 Mustangs with their long range capability were available in quantity for escort duties, and their close presence was a reassuring sight for the bomber crews, as seen through this blister window (right).

gained, pending the availability of the island bases.

First move was the establishment of the 20th Air Force, on 4 April 1944, to which was allocated the XXth Bomber Command and the 58th Bombardment Wing. As their machines became available training was initiated primarily at Salina, Kansas.

Meanwhile, the selection of operational bases in India and China was under way. Southern Bengal was chosen as the Indian rear base area where there already existed many excellent aerodromes that could be adapted for the operation of the Superfortresses. In April and May 1944 the first of the B-29s began to fly in.

In China the difficulties were considerably greater. It was necessary to choose between having advanced bases at minimum range from Japanese targets, or others which were unlikely to be overrun by the Japanese army. The latter course was adopted, the bases being sited in the area of Chengtu, capital of Szechwan province, some 400 miles (643km) from the Hump terminal at Kunming. B-29 bases were to be established at Kiunglai, Kwanghan, Hsinching and Pengshan, the choice taking into consideration the fact that at all but Kwanghan airstrips were already established. To provide air defence, fighter bases were also to be provided at Fenghuan-shan, Kienyang, Pengchiachiang and Shwangliu. The area was almost ideal, for Chengtu lay in the Min River valley where, some 2,000 years earlier, an artificial and highly fertile delta had been created by ingenious irrigation engineering. Covering some 17,000sq miles (44,030sq km) the area was generally level and low lying and also enjoyed fairly good weather for most of the year.

But although airstrips existed at the sites chosen for the B-29s, these had been created for very different aircraft, and needed both lengthening and strengthening for machines which could weigh as much as 70 tons at take-off. The resulting engineering operation was no modern ferro-concrete project utilising the sophisticated tools of the 20th century. Instead, nearly half a million Chinese farmers and peasants wrought a miracle that compared with the Seven Wonders of the ancient world. The tools and techniques they employed were probably similar to those which had created China's Great Wall and so, perhaps, did not seem to them to be at all inadequate to build a mere 8,500ft (2,590m) of paving for each of the Superfortress sites. Each strip was about 1ft 7in (0.48m) thick, the base layer consisting of rounded rocks collected from local streams and river beds. Positioned by hand, they were stabilised by sand and gravel, and were then wetted and rolled by teams of men and women. To provide the hard paving a mixture of clay, crushed rocks, sand and water was spread on the surface of the rolled base layer and this, as it dried in the sun, became similar to adobe or unfired brick. The enormous quantities of materials involved were carried mainly from shoulder yokes, in baskets or buckets, or in wheelbarrows with wooden wheels. Only very occasionally were carts available. It seems hardly possible that the crushed rock was not the product of mechanical crushers, but by the breaking of rock by thousands of hand-held hammers. The 'miracle' was that these huge runways, each with 52 hard standings, were completed less than a month later than originally scheduled. Only the patient Chinese could have created them with such primitive

tools and local raw materials. They were justifiably proud when, on 24 April 1944, the first B-29 landed at Kwanghan; by 10 May all four strips were capable of mounting operations.

It was one thing to have aircraft and airstrips available. Far more complicated was the maintenance of adequate 'over the Hump' supplies for them to become effectively operational. To pinpoint this factor, Maj-Gen Kenneth B. Wolfe, charged initially with the task of strategic bombardment of Japan from the Chinese bases, calculated that two 100-aircraft sorties would require a minimum 4,600 tons of supplies. The only possible solution to such an enormous logistics problem was for the B-29s to accept responsibility for much of their own 'Humping'. Thus a force of 150 stripped B-29s worked endlessly to keep 100 of their number operational.

On 15 June 1944, came the first B-29 strike against Japan proper. The target was the Imperial Iron & Steel Works at Yawata, near the northern tip of Kyushu. 75 aircraft plus two Pathfinders were briefed for the night attack but for various reasons only 47 reached the target area. Of these 15 bombed visually, 32 by radar and by the time all aircraft had landed seven machines and 55 men had been lost. The effort had not been worth the cost for subsequent reconnaissance showed that only one hit had been registered in the target area and that on a power house over half a mile from the all-important coke-ovens. Psychologically it was more effective, making the Japanese population aware that retribution was getting within striking range.

It was important to strike again but quickly. Once again the logistics problem controlled the situation: revert to 'Humping'.

113

But before any significant operations could be mounted against the Japanese, Wolfe was recalled to Washington, promoted to head Materiel Command and, pending posting in of his replacement, Brig-Gen LaVerne G. Saunders assumed command.

The first operation under Saunder's command took place on the night of 7/8 July. Primary targets were the naval dockyard and arsenal at Sasebo and the Akunoura factory at Nagasaki. The 17 aircraft that reached the targets again had little success. One that bombed Sasebo was 15 miles (24km) off target and one of two that aborted and decided to present Hankow with their bombs was 20 miles (32km) in error. Clearly there was much to be put right, and Washington soon began to insist that daylight precision attacks must replace the unproductive and costly night operations.

But before a sizable daylight attack could be mounted there was the inevitable task of Humping. Out of a total of 3,954 tons flown in to prepare for this next mission, Saunders' men accounted for 2,978 tons. Little wonder that fatigue began to affect morale.

On 29 July 107 aircraft were ready for the strike against the Showa steel works at Aushan in Manchuria. Torrential rain washed

Above left: The Liberators begin the liberation: each drop eight 55gal drums of incendiary material on the defences of Iwo Jima.

Left: As soon as the Marines had secured an airstrip on Iwo, P-51s began to fly in to provide defence against enemy counter attack, as well as close support for the Marines.

Above: Soon to be followed by the Mitchells, which had fought their way right across the Pacific.

Centre and bottom right: A surprise visitor was this Sikorsky R-4B, first helicopter produced in quantity for the USAAF which created something of a stir when it touched down on Iwo Jima being the first helicopter seen in the area.

Above: Another new arrival was the Northrop P-61 Black. Widow night fighter, equipped with airborne interception radar and armed with four 0.5in machine guns and four 20mm cannon.

Above right: They proved valuable on Iwo Jima to deal with Japanese intruders and were kept at a constant state of readiness.

Right: Admittedly, their new-fangled electronics were a bit of a nightmare'.

out the Kwanghan strip, so that only 72 Superfortresses got off at the appointed time but the daylight attack proved far more effective and a substantial amount of damage was caused to the target factory.

Another very long-range attack on an oil refinery at Palembang, Sumatra, staged via an RAF base on Ceylon, was to prove yet again that bombing techniques needed considerable improvement. Despite claims of vast explosions and widespread fires, subsequent photo-reconnaissance could establish little more than the destruction of one small building.

In an attempt to find a worthwhile means of seriously disrupting enemy industry, Saunders proposed an incendiary raid on Nagasaki. 24 of 29 machines duly gained the target, but again with insignificant results. Perhaps the highlight of this operation was the recovery of a B-29 that force-landed on a Chinese-held airstrip at Hwaning. Bogged down in cloying mud it suffered damage to two of its engines by Japanese ground strafers. While the necessary spares and mechanics were flown in, the 312th Fighter Wing maintained a non-stop patrol to prevent further enemy action. The brawn and patience of the Chinese, using age-old fulcrum and lever principles, jacked its 35-ton-plus deadweight out of the mud. It was then man-handled to the end of the strip while nearly 5,000 railway sleepers were used to extend the 'runway'. With repairs completed it was eventually flown off to fight another day.

But there was little doubt that the combination of inadequate training, difficult maintenance and a nightmare of a supply situation was far too costly for the very limited results

being achieved. This, then, was the inheritance of Maj-Gen Curtis E. LeMay when he assumed command of XXth Bomber Command on 29 August 1944. Fresh from the European theatre of operations, where heavy bomber deployment against strategic targets had attained devastating efficiency, he brought new drive and a host of ideas.

First and foremost he instituted an intensive training programme, reorganised tactical formations and determined to substitute daylight precision bombing for the night operations that had, until then, produced so little.

In the midst of his training programme, however, came a call to make another strike against the coke-ovens at Aushan. An all-out effort managed to put 109 Superforts into the air on the morning of 26 September, but this time the weather negatived any benefits of the incompleted training. Although 88 machines attacked the primary target, all bombing through the overcast by radar, subsequent reconnaissance showed that no new damage had been caused. It was a continuing aspect of the problems that had plagued heavy bomber operations in the European theatre at an earlier date.

LeMay knew that the primary solution to the problems was intensive training. When renewed activity by the Japanese began to overrun the advanced operating bases in China, causing withdrawal to India, he lost no time in stepping up the essential instruction that he knew would lead to mounting success. There was no doubt that success was needed, for the XXth Bomber Command's 'early sustained bombing of Japan' had been neither early nor sustained. Virtually no strategic advantage had been obtained for a

very considerable expenditure of men, machines and supplies.

Thus began a frustrating period. Although there was a steady build up of strength in India, the crews were soon champing at the bit to have the opportunity of hitting at Japan proper, for there were those who were beginning to think that air power, as represented by the potential of the B-29s, might prove adequate to make unnecessary a costly invasion of the Japanese islands. Experience of the fanatical resistance of the enemy on isolated Pacific islands had left little doubt as to the reception that would be provided for Navy/Marine/Army invasion forces attempting to gain a foothold on the home islands.

India was useless as a base for the B-29s to carry their attack to Japan without forward staging strips. With these denied, at least temporarily, it was essential to operate the VLR bombers from the bases originally considered for their effective deployment: namely the northern Philippines and, more importantly, Saipan in the Marianas. They were, unfortunately, still in enemy hands.

Looking first at the Philippines, aerial reconnaissance had suggested – inaccurately – that Leyete, in the heart of the group, was, free of the enemy. This would provide an ideal base from which to use the XXth's superior air power to subjugate the strongly-held surrounding islands.

On 20 October 1944, unopposed landings were made at the southern tip of Leyete and, despite some enemy resistance, steady progress was made. On 31 October six P-38s of the 7th Fitron were detailed to patrol nearby Tacloban airstrip, and the mission report commented

'As the last P-38 in this flight made his final

approach the pilot, Lt Hill, saw four Vals 50ft overhead preparing to bomb the strip. He evaded the A/A and started to close with a Val which was heading S/W. Approximately 4 miles S/W of the strip, he dove from 600ft to fire a long burst at the Val. He observed hits and saw flames from the left wing root on the Val whose left wing gun started to fire. The Val was then so low as to crash through a telephone line. As Lt Hill pulled up to the left to fire a 30° deflection burst, he saw hits from the engine to behind the canopy. Simultaneously, another P-38 attacked the Val from the right and also scored hits. The Val then exploded and burned . . .'

This was typical of so many combats in the area at that time for, in the main, the Allies had air superiority. Capt John G. Haher reported an earlier combat over Tacloban as follows:
'I was leader of White Flight, consisting of three P-38s patrolling Tacloban . . . at approximately 1600 . . . I sighted six Oscars about 2,000ft above us and about 10 miles south of Tacloban strip. I circled behind them and started to climb after them. When we reached 27,000ft the six Oscars were at 25,000ft. I dove on the tail-end Oscar. He rocked his wings and the leader also rocked his, causing me to hold my fire as I thought they might have been Navy ships. Then the first 4 Oscars chandelled to the left and I saw the red roundels. I started to fire on No 6 Oscar and he half-rolled to the right and split S'd. No 5 Oscar dove to the left. I pulled up and then dove down again on No 6 Oscar. From a tail pass I started a fire in his wing roots and he went down in a spin flaming.

'I chandelled up to the right and saw my wingman, Lt Spruill, starting a diving turn to the right with an Oscar on his tail. I dove on the Oscar and fired about 100 rounds into him and he half-rolled to the right and split S'd under me. I chandelled up and came down on him again and fired another hundred rounds at him. The fight was down to 15,000 (ft) and I closed on his tail. I pressed the trigger and no guns fired . . . all jammed. I dove away from the Nip and headed out to sea and then back to the field, landing at 1615. Maj Bong and Maj Johnson, who watched my last pass, followed the Oscar and Maj Bong shot him down.

'The Oscars were dark green in color. The Nip pilots were experienced and eager to fight.'

These missions were typical of the support provided by the USAAF in these and similar operations, the P-38s providing a fast-moving and effective air umbrella, the medium bombers giving valuable close support and eliminating enemy strong points.

But with American occupation of Leyete threatening to split Japanese strongholds in the Philippines, the enemy were prepared to spare no cost to oust the invaders. This led to the naval battle for Leyete Gulf, one of the most complete naval victories ever recorded and the last occasion that battleships were to be employed in the traditional line of battle formation. The US 3rd and 7th Fleet, commanded respectively by Adm Halsey and Vice-Admiral Kinkaid, decimated the North, Centre and South Japanese naval forces. In the actions of this naval engagement the Japanese lost three battleships, four carriers, ten cruisers and nine destroyers, marking the end of the enemy's once crippling naval power.

Similar desperate tactics were employed in the skies over the Philippines but this activity, also, was to prove a major disaster for the Japanese. In two months of operations over Leyete, USAAF fighter units claimed 314 enemy aircraft destroyed and 45 probables; and Army AA units added 250 destroyed and 110 probables. Among USAAF pilots to gain distinction over Leyete was Maj Richard Bong who, with a total of 38 confirmed victories, was presented with the Congressional Medal of Honor at Tacloban on 12 December 1944, by General MacArthur. In making the presentation MacArthur commented:

'... the Congress of the United States has reserved to itself the honor of decorating those among all who stand out as the bravest of the brave ... It is this highest noble category, Maj Bong, that you now enter as I pin upon your tunic this Medal of Honor. Wear it as a symbol of the invincible courage you have displayed in mortal combat. My dear boy, may a merciful God continue to protect you is the constant prayer of your old Commander-in-Chief.'

Courage and sacrifice of this calibre from all ranks of the US services was displayed in abundance before Leyete was secure. Not only were they fighting a resolute enemy, but a degree of rainfall that threatened to swamp airfields and bog down all surface transport. At Tacloban in November and December 1944 and January 1945 a total rainfall of almost 47 inches (1.19m) was recorded. In consequence Leyete proved a grave disappointment as a major airbase, but units on that island were able to give their support in the operations to seize the island of Mindoro as a stepping stone to Luzon. Air support, provided once again by the 5th and 13th Air Forces and the RAAF, was supplemented by the carrier-based aircraft of Adm William Halsey's task force, and in this campaign for the Philippines every aircraft was to prove vital.

The invasion of Mindoro had been planned originally for 5 December 1944, with the 503rd Parachute Regiment based on Leyete briefed to seize the area of San Jose. However, the slow subjugation of the remainder of Leyete made it appear unlikely that

Left: A patrol of P-61s sets out over the sea as dusk falls.

Below: General view of Iwo Jima on 6 March 1945, after arrival of the P-51s and P-61s.

Right: Iwo received its full share of lame ducks. The propeller of the starboard inboard engine of this B-29 overspeeded, parted company with its shaft, and carved neatly through the fuselage.

Below: This P-61, attempting a blind landing in fog, lost its undercarriage on the P-61 in the background.

Far right: This still-smouldering P-51 was the result of yet another landing collision.

Bottom: Engine failure on take-off wrote off this Mustang. The inevitable 'vultures' soon work over the wreckage for spares.

adequate air support would be available at this date, and a postponement of 10 days was called for. In the interim period efforts were made to reduce the effectiveness of the Japanese aircraft based on Luzon, for they were within such close proximity to Mindoro to cause serious problems during the early stages of the landing. Carrier-based aircraft of the Navy's Task Force 38 attacked Luzon airfields on 14, 15 and 16 December, accounting for almost 270 of an estimated 359 operational aircraft on the island.

At 0730hrs on 15 December combat troops began their first landings on Mindoro, meeting little opposition on the ground, but the gravity of the situation was clear to the enemy and every aircraft which could be coaxed into the air made repeated attacks on the beachhead. Engineers who followed the first batches of troops ashore began

immediately the preparation of two emergency airstrips, named Hill Field and Elmore Field, and within eight days both were operational: within four more days 36th Squadron P-38s, 418th Night Fighter Squadron P-61s, and three of 58th Group's P-47 squadrons were established there.

They arrived none too soon, for on 26 December a naval PB4Y on patrol reported a small Japanese naval force steaming at full speed towards Mindoro. Immediately elements of the 17th and 110th Tactical Reconnaissance Squadrons were flown in to provide additional support, consisting of B-25s and P-40s. Despite a shortage of bombs on the island, and the difficulty of operating by night from the newly-established and soft strips, a determined assault was mounted by 13 B-25s, 44 P-38s, 20 P-40s and 28 P-47s. At 1940hrs they swept in to the attack, switching on navigation lights as they completed their run to avoid collision in the dark. Many landed twice at Mindoro to rearm and refuel, throwing everything they had at the Japanese, but with few bombs they were unable to inflict serious damage on the battleship, heavy cruiser and six destroyers of which the enemy force was comprised. So spirited was their attack however, that most of the enemy's guns were silenced, their gun crews dead or dying, and the attackers succeeded only in sinking one Liberty ship and causing some damage to the landing strip at Hill Field before making their withdrawal, Unable to risk a landing at Hill Field in the dark, many pilots headed for Leyete, but with fuel tanks almost drained or with damaged aircraft, not all gained this haven. Losses totalled 26 aircraft, almost 25% of those engaged, but their sacrifice had prevented the Japanese from eliminating the newly-established beachhead. Brig-Gen W. C. Dunckel in command on Mindoro was to comment later: 'The action of our air units on that night will stand forever as one of the most gallant deeds ... established in the traditions of American fighting men.'

Mindoro was secure, but the enemy continued to mount air strikes in an attempt to dislodge the Americans from the island, and launched *kamikaze* attacks against shipping endeavouring to bring in urgently needed supplies. Stocks of aviation fuel dwindled to a point where only defensive sorties could be flown from 30 December, and rations were getting desperately low. Special efforts were made to reverse this situation so that the units on Mindoro could play their appointed role in the invasion of Luzon, scheduled for 9 January 1945, and nearly 5,000 drums of fuel were airlifted in by 8 January, and a Navy service group supplemented this by some 10,000 barrels.

Japanese airfields in Luzon were attacked

Top left: Iwo Jima also provided a first class base for air-sea rescue craft. This ASR B-17 carries a lifeboat to drop to ditched crews.

Above left: A B-17 ASR machine on patrol, seeking a crew reported down off Chichi Jima, Bonin Islands. Aircraft dinghies were minute targets to find in these almost limitless expanses of open sea.

Left: Thunderbolts taxi from dispersal to take off point, guided by a ground crew member on the port wing. Without such guidance the pilot was forced to swing the big fighter from side to side to get a forward view, no easy task on taxi tracks such as this.

Above: The moment arrives to strike back at the Philippines. P-38 Lightnings drop napalm containers on Luzon.

continually by Allied aircraft from Leyete and Mindoro, by bombers staging through Leyete, and by carrier-based aircraft of Halsey's Task Force 38. A serious problem was to ensure that, so far as possible, the friendly civilian population was unharmed, calling for accurate attack on the primary targets: Clark, Nichols and Nielson Fields. The biggest effort, and what proved to be the largest co-ordinated operation by light and medium bombers in the Southwest Pacific area, was mounted on 7 January, supplemented by the efforts of Halsey's aircraft. B-25s of the 345th Group and A-20s of the 312th and 417th Groups made an accurate attack on Clarke field despite low cloud, dropping nearly 8,000 fragmentation bombs on that one target. Inspection and enquiry at the three main airfields, following capture of Luzon, showed that in just four months more than 1,500 Japanese aircraft had been put out of action on the ground by these and earlier attacks. When it was most needed by the Japanese, as US forces went ashore on the beaches of Lingayen, their island-based air defence was non-existent.

The landings on the Lingayen beaches, at 0930hrs on 9 January 1945, proceeded as planned without great difficulty, and only

occasional air attacks were made by the Japanese, apparently from the direction of Formosa. Within six days the Japanese were committed to fight without any air support; and to limit any further air strikes from afar, airfields on Formosa and Okinawa were blasted by B-29s of XX Bomber Command.

But although there was little combat in the air, the fierce resistance of the enemy on the ground called for large scale help from both USAAF and Navy aircraft. 5th Air Force aircraft found new and rewarding results from interdiction sorties, destroying bridges, locomotives, rolling stock and transport vehicles, but as the Army forged ahead against fanatical resistance the demand for air reconnaissance and close support grew rapidly. From then until early March, when the capital of the Philippines – Manila – was purged of the Japanese, air support was provided on a non-stop basis. And with Manila secure and clearing-up operations in progress, tons of high explosive was used to shatter the Japanese in strongholds such as the mountainous Bataan and the strongly fortified island of Corregidor. Benumbed by the weight of such attacks, the survivors were then flushed from their caves and

Above: Airborne troops helped seize the vital Appari airstrip on Luzon. Waco CG-15A gliders of the 11th Airborne Division are seen after landing in north Luzon.

Right: Individual ambulance services were provided by Stinson L-5 Sentinels. This one is en route to a forward strip at Linga, Maguna de Bay, Luzon.

foxholes by napalm bombs: as they fled in terror from the flames they were torn to shreds by machine gun fire, and thousands died before Luzon could be considered secure.

The original plan had been to bypass the other Philippine islands, most of which had enemy garrisons, but which had been reduced in numbers and effectiveness by air attack. The fact that they could be dominated by aircraft operating from the well-established bases on Luzon suggested that further action against them was unnecessary: with little chance of them being reinforced, or of receiving supplies by sea or air, they presented little threat. However, Gen MacArthur considered there were considerations other than purely military which dictated the Japanese should be cleared from the Netherlands East Indies, Borneo and the remaining occupied Philippine islands. These tasks, in the main, fell to the Australians with support from the

USAAF and US Navy, but even then in some areas Japanese resistance did not end until the surrender in August. Nevertheless, on 5 July 1945 Gen MacArthur declared the campaign for the Philippine islands at an end. True to his promise of early 1942, the Americans had returned.

Earlier in 1944, however, events of even greater significance for future operations had been taking place in an area some 1,250 miles (2,010km) east of the Philippines where, after a decision to by-pass Truk Atoll, plans had been prepared to occupy the Marianas islands of Saipan, Guam and Tinian.

15 June 1944 was D-Day for Saipan, and pre-invasion naval and air bombardment had been maintained from 11 June. This had been so successful that the Marines were able to make their initial landings with little difficulty; it was only when they attempted to advance that they encountered bitter resistance from the Japanese, who had

retreated to prepared and strongly fortified positions. Equally determined the Marines, now supported by an infantry division, pushed ahead to capture Aslito (subsequently renamed Isley) airfield. This allowed a squadron of P-47s to come in and provide the all-essential close support, creating hell on earth for the enemy by strafing them with rockets, bombs, napalm and the full force of their eight 0.5in machine guns. By 9 July all organised resistance on the island had ended, although pockets of fanatical defenders were still being rounded up when the war ended, over 12 months later.

With close-range air support available from Saipan, the islands of Tinian and Guam were subjected to a non-stop air attack, supplementing intensive naval bombardment. And to enhance the air support, B-25s of the 48th Bombardment Squadron were moved forward to Saipan. Their 75mm cannon proved particularly effective in low-level attacks on enemy positions and when, in early August, the three main islands were considered secure, they and the P-47s were able to turn their attention to neutralisation of Japanese garrisons on the surrounding lesser islands of the Marianas.

At last had arrived the moment for which so much planning had been carried out. Within days, engineers and equipment began to pour into the newly-won islands, for these were to be the all-important bases from which the Superforts would carry devastation to the Japanese home islands. Eventually five vast airfields were completed, one on Saipan and two each on Guam and Tinian. It had been the original intention for Saipan, the nearest

to Japan, to have two bases, but ground survey of the island proved this to be impossible.

But despite the urgent need to make these bases operational at the earliest moment, it was almost five months before the first B-29 was to be put down on Isley Field. Biggest problem had been the weather, with tropical storms so intense during July and August that the unsurfaced roads became impassable. The only solution was to divert practically all men and equipment to building hard-surfaced roads to speed the transit of coral from quarries to runway surfaces. Some indication of the scope of this project is given by the fact that, eventually, Isley Field had two 9,000ft by 200ft (2,743m by 610m) runways, 200 hard standings, service and warm-up aprons, taxiways, road, fuel and bomb storage, housing and facilities for personnel. All built on a coral island, some 5,750 miles (9,255km) distant from the nearest point on the continental US. Tinian's first strip became operational just before the end of the year, and that on Guam on 2 February 1945.

On 12 October 1944, the first B-29 came sweeping over the airfield on Saipan, complete with fighter escort. A USAAF historian recorded that; '. . . a great cheer went up, and all work stopped as men shaded their eyes to watch the plane pass over . . . The thrill that went through all was almost electric with effect.'

This first Superfort on the Marianas, named *Joltin' Josie*, was flown by Brig-Gen Haywood S. Hansell Jr, who had been placed in command of the XXst Bomber Command on 29 August. He had a formidable

Above left: The L-5s operating on Luzon were supported by the much rarer Noorduyn C-64 Norseman. A Canadian-built utility aircraft, small numbers were used by the USAAF and could ferry three litter patients.

Above: Fighting was bitter and P-47s and P-51s operating from Tacloban Airstrip, Leyete, hit the enemy hard. Maj William Dunham, seen here, accounted for two Japanese 'Zekes' and two 'Oscars' in one sortie. He was to end a distinguished career in the Air Force as Brig-Gen Dunham, Vice-Commander of the USAAF 3rd Air Force.

task ahead of him before the first B-29 raids could be mounted against Japan. Primary problem was the slow receipt of his bomber force, planned to be ferried from Mather Field, California, via Honolulu and Kwajalein at a rate of five aircraft per day. But even the best laid plans seldom materialised and with receipt of only two or three aircraft per day, Hansell was considerably short of the planned initial strength of 180 B-29s. By 22 November, two days before the first scheduled mission over Japan, he had received only 118.

Prime need, however, whatever the size of the force, was combat training. Pacific weather, long ranges and aggressive Japanese defences were a very different proposition to practice flights in the peaceful skies of the US. Hansell elected to use Truk Atoll as his training target, for it offered a fairly long distance flight, indoctrination with the vagaries of Pacific weather, plus the likelihood of moderate anti-aircraft defence from the reduced garrison at Truk. It was not until 28 October that 18 Superforts trundled off Saipan's runway to begin their first shakedown flight.

As a training mission it proved only moderately successful. Four aircraft aborted, and the 14 that unloaded their bombs from

25,000ft (7,620m) on the Dublon submarine pens at Truk, managed to get only a small percentage of their bombs anywhere near the target. But it was a start and Truk was to continue as the primary training target for newly arrived combat units until the end of the war.

Hansell followed up the initial training flight to Truk with two others, on 30 October and 2 November. The bombing results were even less impressive. And when on 5 November he sent his force against the more formidable target of Iwo Jima, only about 25% of their bombs were within 1,000ft (305m) of the aiming point.

But by then the first planned strike on Tokyo was less than three weeks distant. A primary weakness lay in the fact that USAAF planners had no recent reconnaissance photo coverage of potential targets in Japan. In fact, to put it crudely, no US aircraft had been over Tokyo since Doolittle's B-25s on 18 April 1942. The need to gain some appreciation of changed conditions was clear to all, but it was not until the arrival at Saipan on 30 October of two F-13As that the problem could be tackled.

The F-13As were reconnaissance versions of the B-29, provided with K-18 and K-22 cameras, and with auxiliary fuel tanks in the bomb bay to give extreme long range. Two days later one of these was cruising at 32,000ft (9,755m) over Tokyo, its cameras busy recording important detail during a flight which occupied nearly 14 hours. These reconnaissance machines, soon increased in number, were to find their spy task fairly trouble free. Enemy fighter and anti-aircraft fire presented no serious opposition. Their greatest enemy was the weather, as a result of which only some 30% of their missions were effective.

D-Day for the first attack on Tokyo was set for 17 November 1944, and long before the appointed take-off time the whole of Saipan was a hive of activity. It has been commented that the impending operation was a well-known secret. The number of war correspondents and photographers that arrived to record the triumphant mission to the Japanese homeland confirmed this to be true. Then came anti-climax. Local weather was too bad to despatch the avenging fleet.

Left: Naturally, the enemy reacted as hard as their diminishing means would allow, leaving this P-38 of little use to the scavengers at Tacloban Airstrip.

Below: Meanwhile, strength had been building up on the Marianas in preparation for LeMay's all-out attack on Japan. A batch of new P-47s awaiting assembly on Guam.

Left: In combat with enemy fighters, this P-38 was hit hard by a 'Zeke'. Its pilot, Lt S.F. Ford, crash-landed at Mandano and was photographed as he staggered away from the wreckage of his Lightning.

Right: Fresh air storage on Guam for new Wright R-3350 radial engines to power the B-29s.

And so it remained for a whole week until at 0615hrs on 24 November the first Superfort trundled down the runway. with Brigadier General 'Rosey' O'Donnel at the controls. Heavily loaded with fuel and bombs it used almost every inch of runway, skimmed the coral reef and climbed slowly out of sight.

In all, 111 B-29s took the air, and of these 17 aborted en route and six were unable to release their bombs because of technical defects. The remainder found the inevitable weather problems over the target and a 138 mph (222km/h) wind at their bombing altitude. Not surprisingly, they caused little damage to their target, Nakajima's aero-engine plant, and which was found after the war to have suffered only 1% damage to buildings and 2.4% to the productive machinery.

Enemy defence was far below what had been anticipated and B-29 crews claimed seven enemy fighters destroyed and 18 probables. USAAF losses totalled two machines, one rammed by an enemy fighter and one which was forced to ditch on the way home when it ran out of fuel.

This was to remain very much the pattern of the daylight high-altitude attacks which followed until, on 13 December, 90 aircraft took off to attack the Mitsubishi aero-engine works at Nagoya. On this occasion the bombing results showed considerable improvement, with some 18% of the buildings being destroyed. This success prompted Hansell to strike at the same company's aircraft works, also at Nagoya, on 18 December, and they were to record a very similar degree of destruction.

It will be recalled that Maj-Gen LeMay's XXth Bomber Command had achieved some success with their incendiary attack on Hankow, and there was considerable pressure for Hansell to try a similar raid on the Japanese homeland where, it was believed,

incendiary attack would cause widespread destruction.

Accordingly, on 3 January 1945, a force of 90 Superforts set off for Nagoya, each machine well laden with incendiary clusters. Visibility was again bad over the target, and when crews found smoke at 20,000ft (6,100m) they assumed their attack to have met with considerable success. Then, only the citizens of Nagoya new otherwise.

It was not until 19 January that the XXIst met with their first real success, when 62 B-29s dropped their load of high explosive bombs on the Kawasaki aircraft factory at Akashi. Subsequent reconnaissance indi-

cated that the factory had been well and truly hit, but it was only after the war that it became known that production had been reduced to a trickle of around 10%.

It was something of a crowning achievement for Hansell's precision daylight attacks, but was to be the last under his command. Upper echelons of Air Force staff, bursting at the seams to see the strategic bombers knock the heart out of Japan's productive capacity, had lost patience at what they considered Hansell's slow approach. He was recalled to the US and to LeMay fell the task of directing this great air armada to destroy the factories and cities of the enemy.

Left: Before he could begin to clobber Japan, LeMay had to be involved in the frustrating but highly successful mining operations. A Superfort dropping mines over Japanese home waters.

Below left: The bomb load of a B-29 of the 314th Bomb Wing, based on Guam, is readied for a strike on Tokyo.

Right: En route to the target, the Superforts were then able to collect escorting P-51s over Iwo Jima. The much reduced range for the fighters meant they could adopt far more aggressive tactics against Japanese defences.

Below: An almost non-stop attack against Japanese targets became routine. A pre-strike reconnaissance photograph of Otake refinery (left), and the same target enjoying the full benefit of B-29 attack (right).

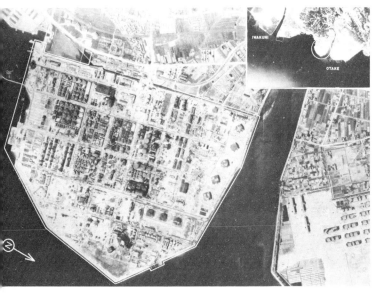

8
The
Whirlwind

Right: An important base in preparation for the elimination of all Japanese resistance, especially if the normal amphibious invasion was necessary, was Okinawa. Its principal city, Naha, was gutted in pre-invasion strikes.

Maj-Gen Curtis E. LeMay was a man who believed in action. Within a short space of time he had brought new spirit to the men of the XXth Bomber Command in the CBI. The limited number of aircraft available, and the ever-present restriction on all kinds of supplies imposed by the 'Hump' route, were things that even his exuberance could do little to rectify.

He arrived at Saipan determined that his new XXIst Bomber Command should show the world the meaning of air power. Here he was assisted by a supply organisation in the US that backed him to the hilt, for direct attack on the Japanese homeland was the prime wish of practically every living and breathing American. Furthermore, the 'Hump' was eliminated, replaced by an ever-growing naval force that could bring the fuel, weapons and spares needed to hit the enemy so hard that he would have little chance of making any significant counter-attack.

This, then, was the glowing spirit in which he arrived to tackle what he knew would be a difficult but more than worthwhile job.

But before he had left, Hansell had listed what he considered the major problems:

Above and left: LeMay's low-level night incendiary raids were to spell the destruction of Japan's cities, large and small. The early stages of an attack on Tokyo on the night of 26 May 1945 (above) and the post-attack desolation of Japan's capital city (left).

Right: Retribution falls like rain from the skies as the Superforts unload their incendiaries in a daylight raid over Yokohama (above) and the scene below as the first bombs begin to strike home (right).

'deplorable' bombing accuracy, an abort rate in excess of 20%, plans to convert the force from a night radar bombing group to precision daylight attacks, and a desperate need to reduce the number of ditchings and improve air-sea rescue.

Nevertheless, LeMay was anxious to mount some early operations to gain first hand experience of the problems in this theatre. On 23 January, of a total of 73 Superforts sent against Nagoya, only 28 bombed the target, obscured by 9/10ths cloud. An attack on the Musashina district of Tokyo four days later was even less successful, the target completely hidden by clouds the B-29s hustled along at a ground-related speed of nearly 500mph (805km/h) as they became embroiled in high-altitude jet streams.

It was vital to establish a pattern of attack that would enable the Superforts to cause major damage when conditions were such that they could operate over the target without too many meteorological setbacks. It was decided to mount a large scale incendiary strike on Kobe, which was Japan's sixth largest city and a major port. A highly industrial area with congested business and factory districts, it was considered a target

that should offer considerable scope for fire-raising tactics.

By the time that favourable weather forecasts enabled LeMay to name 3 February as the date of the mission, he had a total of 129 Superforts available, and of these 69 got through to Kobe to deliver over 150 tons of incendiary weapons. It proved a far more successful attack than that on Nagoya, and postwar information revealed that damage was considerably in excess of that claimed by intelligence officers following photo-reconnaissance. Over 1,000 buildings were destroyed and more than 4,000 people rendered homeless. More importantly, local production was hit severely and two major shipyards had their output halved.

While LeMay continued to launch operations of moderate size, mixing targets and weapons to keep the enemy off balance as much as possible, came the invasion of Iwo Jima. This was not only highly desirable to provide a base even nearer to the Japanese homeland, but offered a solution to the many ditchings of B-29s by providing an intermediate staging post that could be used in case of fuel shortage or more dire emergency. It offered also an outward bound staging post, a site for navigational aids and a base for fighter escorts as well as for air-sea rescue units. And since it was at that time an operational Japanese airfield on which between 100 and 200 aircraft were based, it posed a distinct threat to the US Marianas bases if the Japanese felt disposed to attack them.

Left and below : These two pictures show bombs almost filling the sky as they fall in a daylight raid on Osaka.

Right : These two show Kobe during and immediately after an attack.

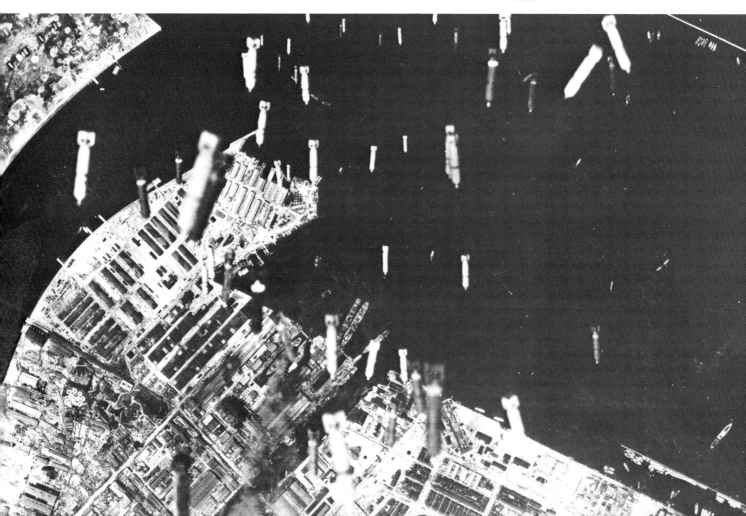

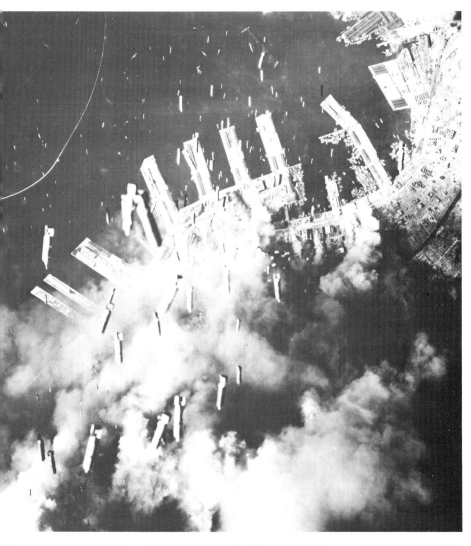

In fact, during November and December they did feel so inclined, and a number of small scale attacks were launched. The most damaging were against Isley Field where, by Christmas Day, they had accumulated a total of about a dozen B-29s destroyed on the ground and 50 damaged. The time had come to eliminate this constant source of annoyance and, at the same time, gain the very tangible benefits of the island base.

It featured also in considerations other than the B-29 operations against Japan, for Admiral Nimitz was insistent that prior to the invasion of Okinawa and the Bonins an advanced island base capable of supporting several airstrips was essential. Only Iwo would meet this requirement.

It was known that the Japanese had established heavy fortifications on the island and a necessary prelude to invasion was a very thorough softening up by naval and air bombardment. Even then a three- or four-day large scale battle was anticipated. This proved to be one of the all-time underestimates of US planners.

On 31 January, 7th Air Force Liberators started the ball rolling and they alone, by 16 February, had dropped some 600 tons of bombs and more than 1,000 napalm containers on the Japanese defences. LeMay's B-29s added limited support and on 16 February navy battleships and cruisers began to pound the island with their heavy guns. Air strikes from escort carriers added their quota and on D-Day, 19 February, a total of seven battleships and nineteen cruisers put over a concentration of fire that should have ensured elimination of the defences. In fact it was argued subsequently, with some justification, that the protracted period of softening up, extending over nearly three weeks, had given the enemy ample time to extend and strengthen their underground fortifications.

When the Marines went ashore at 0900hrs their initial landings were reasonably successful, and by nightfall almost 30,000 had been put ashore. It seemed that complete ejection of the Japanese would be only a matter of days. Top brass could not have been more wrong, for it was not until almost a month later, on 16 March, that the island could be considered securely in the hands of the Americans. Even then, isolated pockets of fanatical defenders were to prove a constant problem.

Iwo Jima must forever remain a memorial to the supreme courage of the US Marine Corps, and one of their all time outstanding battles. Their casualties numbered nearly 21,000 of which 4,590 were killed. They, in return killed over 21,000 Japanese. There were those who were to question whether the cost had been worthwhile. The unequi-

Above: Once on Okinawa the first task, as usual, was the construction of the airstrips needed for large-scale operations. Awase Airstrip, Okinawa, under construction by the 36th Naval Construction Battalion.

Above right: One of the first arrivals on Okinawa was this Douglas A-26B Invader of the 48th Bomb Squadron. Carrying ten 0.5in machine guns, able to lift 4,000lb (1,815kg) of bombs and capable of 355mph (571km/h) it was a formidable light bomber.

Below: A Liberator of the 11th Bomb Group takes off from Yontan Airstrip, Okinawa, in the early days of occupation. Note the task force in the harbour, the scene of the first landings.

Right: P-38 Lightnings of the 8th Photo Reconnaissance Squadron on Motabu Airstrip, Okinawa. Most senior of the Pacific photo-reconnaissance units, they had worked their passage across the Pacific, from Australia to the skies over Japan.

Above: Okinawa bases made Japanese targets something of a milk-run for the Liberators. Here machines of the 90th and 380th Bomb Groups are being readied for a raid.

Left: Alongside them worked the ever-faithful P-47s. This Thunderbolt – *Jane* – is given VIP treatment by 318th Fighter Group armourers in preparation for an escort sortie.

Above right: Ie Shima, an island just off Okinawa, complete with its US airstrips.

Right: The final destination is nailed to the totem-style signpost erected on Ie Shima.

vocal answer must be yes, for Iwo was to prove an invaluable base. To take a single argument for the credit side, by the end of the war some 2,400 B-29s had made emergency landings on its runways, representing a haven for a crew total of 25,000 men. Admittedly, the availability of this mid-sea airfield was often used as one of convenience by less-spirited crews who, in its absence, would have pushed on and gained their home bases at Saipan, Guam or Tinian. Nevertheless, it is reasonable to assume that its availability saved the lives of considerably more airmen than the total of Marines lives given to its capture.

In addition, of course, it provided an excellent base for air-sea rescue services and which, co-ordinated with submarines, surface vessels, seaplanes and specially-equipped B-17s and B-29, gave a steadily-improving rescue service for those unfortunate enough to end up in waters that were, generally, far from 'pacific'. Two statistics will serve to illustrate the increasing efficiency of such rescue services in these closing stages of the war: known losses at sea in January 1945 totalled 125 men in 649 sorties, by July they numbered only 47 men in 5,536 sorties. There was little doubt, too, that the psychological reassurance of such a standard of air-sea rescue, plus the availability of the mid-ocean airfield at Iwo Jima, did much for the morale of those men committed to the daily grind from the Marianas to Japan and back.

139

Right: Not all the offensive flights were against the enemy. This Douglas C-47 operating over Okinawa is busy with a spray mission to reduce the malarial mosquitoes that abounded there.

Below: Air power mounting against the enemy began to assume overpowering proportions. Lines of Douglas C-54 Skymasters of Air Transport Command's 13th Air Cargo Re-Supply Squadron on Okinawa's Kadena Airfield.

But even with such an insurance policy to hearten his men, LeMay was still faced with the inescapable fact that his strategic force was making no serious inroads into Japanese productive capacity or morale. As late as 6 March 1945, he had commented that: 'This outfit had been getting a lot of publicity without having really accomplished a hell of a lot in bombing results'. It was a justifiable gripe, but the reasons for failure were multiple and complex.

First and foremost, the USAAF had long been wedded to an inflexible policy for its strategic bombers of daylight precision bombardment, relying upon heavy defensive armament for protection against enemy fighters. When their first 11 B-17 daylight operations in the European theatre had suffered the loss of only two Fortresses, it had seemed that their concept was right. Only later in the war were questions to arise when it became apparent that long-range penetration of German airspace was unacceptably costly without strong fighter escort. The

correct assumption that Japanese defences would not prove as strong as those of the Germans, plus the greater speed, ceiling and firepower of the B-29s, seemed to require no modifications to the original concept for which they had been created.

In opposition to such beliefs, operations with the B-29s had shown that unpredictable weather, high speed winds at the operational altitude of the Superforts, spirited fighter defence and the disappointing results of 'precision' bombing had resulted so far, in little achievement at considerable cost.

LeMay postulated that a completely new re-think was necessary. Why not, he suggested, switch to night attack, when cloud cover seemed to thin out; when enemy intercepters would pose no real threat: and when the rather unsophisticated anti-aircraft defence would be at its least effective.

It made sense, a great deal of sense, the only real weakness being that the force was not really trained for night operations. No doubt that could be overcome by utilising a

272423

THE AIR TRANSPORT COMMA

Top: The close range of the Okinawa air bases from Japan meant that occasional enemy suicide attacks could pay off. This 'Betty' force-landed on Yontan airstrip carrying a demolition squadron of suicide troops. **Above:** They managed to cause considerable damage to parked aircraft before being wiped out.

Right: But this P-47 of the 464th Fighter Squadron was not hit by the enemy. Its pilot mistook a taxiway for a runway and crashed during a night landing on Ie Shima.

Pathfinder group for initial target illumination.

So far, so good. LeMay's next proposals were far more controversial. Concentrate on incendiary attack; make the flights at low level; and strip the B-29s of defensive armament. The first point could be swallowed without too much difficulty, for there was already general agreement that Japan's towns and cities would suffer more from fire than high explosive, and the two small-scale incendiary raids on Hankow and Kobe had proved to be two of the most damaging of the war.

Low level attack was a very different proposition, quite contrary to the design specification of the B-29. LeMay's arguments in favour of the low level mission included greater accuracy, unaffected by the high

altitude jet streams, a heavier bomb load and increased engine life. He could offer no guarantee against the possibility that low level attack might increase considerably the loss of aircraft to anti-aircraft defences. His only counter to this argument was that initially, at any rate, the enemy would be caught on the wrong foot, having become accustomed to high altitude US attacks, and that heavier bomb loads dropped more accurately should saturate the defences to a point of inefficiency.

His third point, to strip the B-29s of defensive armament was more than heretical. No longer would his aircraft be Superfortresses; instead, if they survived, they would at best be Superbombers. But his argument was more than logical, for with the expectation of little, if any, fighter oppo-

sition in early attacks, each of his bombers would be able to carry an additional 3,000lb (1,360kg) of incendiaries.

The pros and cons were argued by day and night. In the final analysis LeMay carried the make or break decision on his own shoulders, committing his force to a series of high-intensity incendiary raids that would prove once and for all if the end justified the risks involved.

The first raid was set for the night of 9/10 March 1945, and by the time the force was assembled a total of 334 B-29s stood by for take-off; their combined bomb load something over 2,000 tons, their target Tokyo.

The first machines lifted off from Guam at 1735hrs, those from Saipan and Tinian at 1815hrs, but it was not until 2020hrs that all of the force was airborne, heading out through heavy cloud and turbulence to their target more than 1,600 miles (2,575km) distant. It was uneventful trip and, as had been forecast, weather conditions improved near Tokyo, the Pathfinders having little difficulty in finding their aiming points, which were soon illuminated for the following force by nicely burning fires.

As load after load of incendiaries went hurtling down into the chaotic conditions below the flames, fanned into a holocaust by natural and heat-induced winds, spread like a bush fire among the wood-and-bamboo housing, engulfing even those buildings of conventional fire-resistant construction.

As had been anticipated the defences, both military and civil, were overwhelmed, for the change in tactics had caught them unprepared. Anti-aircraft defence was largely ineffective and mostly inaccurate, and not a single bomber fell to fighter defences. Subsequent analysis revealed a loss ratio of 4.2%, comparing favourably with an average 5.7% during January, a month in which no significant results had been achieved.

Looking back on their target as they headed for their island bases, the crews had the almost indescribable sight of a vast city completely engulfed in flames: even from a distance of 150 miles (240km) it was still visible. Checked only by the wide fire-breaks of rivers, fire had reduced 15.8sq miles (40.92sq km) to ashes; 18% of the industrial area, and 63% of the commercial area and the heart of the densely-packed residential district had gone. The official death toll was 83,793; another 40,918 had been injured and 1,008,005 persons rendered homeless. It remains the world's most devastating air attack of all time. Many who sought to escape from the certain death of flame jumped into the city's canals, only to perish in water that had already been raised near to boiling point. A Japanese official commented later: 'People were unable to escape. They were found later

Below: The all-out attacks in the final stages covered all types of targets. B-25 Mitchells equipped with Mk13 torpedoes became torpedo-bombers in attacks against enemy shipping.

Bottom: Mitchells of the 47th Bomb Squadron, 41st Bomb Group set out from Okinawa to attack Saseba Harbour, Kyusuhu.

Above right: This attack on Kanoya East Airfield by P-51 Mustangs shows one enemy defence against low-level fighters. The black ground bursts are from electrically detonated land mines, their blast intended to engulf the attacking fighters.

Below right: Through the Pacific War, as in the European theatre, petroleum was a vital strategic target. A B-25 of the 5th Air Force photographed during an attack on the oil refinery at Koyagi Shima.

piled upon the bridges, roads, and in the canals, 80,000 dead . . . We were instructed to report on actual conditions. Most of us were unable to do so because of horrifying conditions beyond imagination.'

LeMay's gamble had brought unbelievable success, and similar attacks were mounted on Nagoya (11 March), Osaka (13 March), Kobe (16 March), and Nagoya again on 19 March. In these initial raids 1,595 B-29 sorties dropped no less than 9,365 tons of incendiary bombs on these four cities, and the resulting 32sq miles (83sq km) of destruction proved that LeMay's new tactics had the potential to destroy the enemy's will to continue the war. Indeed, this was confirmed by a number of statements made postwar. Toshikazu Kase, an advisor in the Japanese Foreign Office, was to comment of these attacks, 'Panic seized the people. A frantic and disorderly exodus from major cities took place. Chaos prevailed and public morale collapsed. The Diet was then in

session, and though debates and discussions were muffled, its temper was rising against the Cabinet. For, try as it might, the government could no longer conceal the realities of the situation.'

This particular statement is most interesting, for it confirms that prior to these major raids on the Japanese homelands, government propaganda had been able to convince the population of the nation that all was well. The B-29 raids made by XXIst Bomber Command made them realise for the first time the true horror of war, and that the Japanese Empire was most certainly not invincible.

For the remainder of March the attacks were to continue, but at a much reduced intensity. Two factors were responsible for this: an acute shortage of incendiary weapons, which these early raids had consumed at a rate far in excess of logistics planning; and the need to contribute towards the impending invasion of Okinawa, while other

elements of the 5th Air Force began to neutralise airfields on Formosa.

Formosa was a vital Japanese possession, industrially well developed so that it provided a significant contribution to Japan's requirements for butanol (produced from sugar cane and an important constituent of aviation fuel), aluminium, copper and iron: there were also oil refineries in the island. Situated in the East China Sea, some 700 miles (1,127km) south-west of Kyushu, and only about 300 miles (483km) north of Luzon, it had represented a staging post en route to the Empire's new conquests. And because of this importance, it had some 50 airstrips, to cater both for aircraft staging through, as well as to provide defence for the island and support for operations in the Philippines.

During 1943 there had been some small-scale air attacks against the island, but it was not until late 1944 and early 1945 that XXth Bomber Command in conjunction with Admiral Halsey's Third Fleet began to

pound Formosa, to reduce its support for the Japanese then fighting to throw the Americans off the beachhead at Luzon. In January 1945 the 5th Air Force could only make token attacks against Formosa, as the majority of its efforts was needed in support of the campaign in the Philippines. The result was that small forces sent over the island had to face a daunting ground and air defence. Typical was that experienced by Lt Albert J. Goossens and his crew in a B-24, one of three despatched by the 63rd Squadron to attack Takao on the night of 30 January 1945.

Goossens' aircraft was second over the target and in no time was picked up and held by searchlights as it made its bomb run towards fuel storage tanks. Bombing was accurate, four fires starting immediately and these, in no time at all, were one huge conflagration. The bombs had not gone a moment too soon, for even before the Liberator's bomb doors began to close an anti-aircraft shell exploded in the bomb bay: as the doors slammed to a second shell

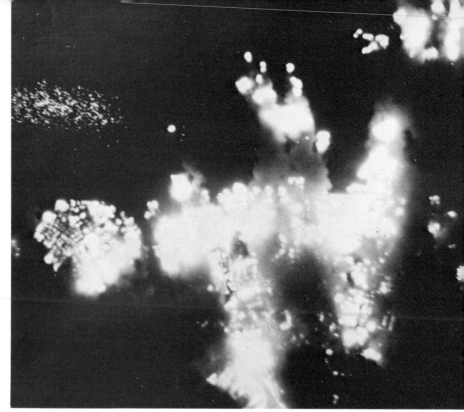

Left: XXIst Bomber Command concentrated on the destruction of enemy production potential and morale. Fire spreading throughout Shizuoka on the night of 12 July 1945.

Below left: By the following morning 66% of the city had been destroyed.

Right: A spectacular explosion on Kagamigahara.

Below: Superforts unloading incendiary weapons over Hitashi.

ripped through them, and a third tore the cowlings from the starboard inner engine. Inside the aircraft Goossens and his co-pilot, 2-Lt Charles Phippen, struggled to regain control: but as they managed to get on an even keel and pull away from the target area bullets came slamming in from the rear as seven Japanese night fighters decided they had found an easy number.

For the next few minutes all hell was let loose as the night fighters attacked from the stern and flanks. Tail gunner S/Sgt Charles Trusty sent one of the Japanese fighters spinning down in flames before being injured by cannon fire: S/Sgt Bruce Willingham dragged him amidships and took over the tail position to such effect that he, too, was able to claim the destruction of an enemy fighter. Almost immediately the remaining waist gunner, who had been doing his best to maintain bursts of fire from both waist guns, was hit in the arm by a bullet, and Willingham came back to dress his wound before scoring hits on a third attacker. By then Goossens had got the B-24 down to almost 1,000ft (305m) to seek cloud cover, but a final burst from one of the Japanese fighters hit their starboard outer engine as they slipped into the clouds.

They had escaped the enemy, but were in a parlous state. The hydraulic system and automatic pilot were not functioning which meant that, assuming they reached an airstrip, flaps and landing gear would be inoperable except by a hand system – if it still worked: in any event there would be no brakes. Their starboard outer engine had been put out of action by the enemy's last attack: presumably a bullet had clipped the hose of the feathering pump, as the large propeller could not be feathered and was windmilling in the slipstream. An alternative suggestion was that the engine had lost all of its oil, so that the feathering pump was starved, and this proved to be the case, for not long afterwards the engine, overheated by the windmilling propeller, ceased up and burst into flames. By a miracle the entire propeller span off its shaft and fell away without causing further damage, and shortly after the fire burned itself out. Now it was possible to proceed with a little more purpose.

The nearest suitable airstrip was that at Lingayen, on Luzon, and permission was given to land there – subject to a Japanese air raid then in progress not causing such damage that it would be impossible to put the big Liberator down there. After stooging around off the coast, waiting for the Japanese to clear off, Goossens and his co-pilot managed to get flaps and landing gear down by using the hand pump. Making their approach to the searchlight illuminated strip they concentrated on getting the wheels down within the first few feet, prepared for a long

Left: A post-strike photograph shows huge areas of Hitashi reduced to cinders.

Below left: The Mitsubishi aircraft factory at Nagoya had long been a priority target. It, too, was eliminated by incendiary attack.

Right: XXIst Bomber Command's potential was awesome. A total of 5,424 tons of incendiaries were dropped on Kobe, the principal port of Japan.

Below: Toyama, an important centre of aluminium production, was literally burned out on the night of 1 August 1945, with almost 96% of the city demolished. A Japanese official commented: 'Panic seized the people. A frantic and disorderly exodus from major cities took place. Chaos prevailed and public morale collapsed.'

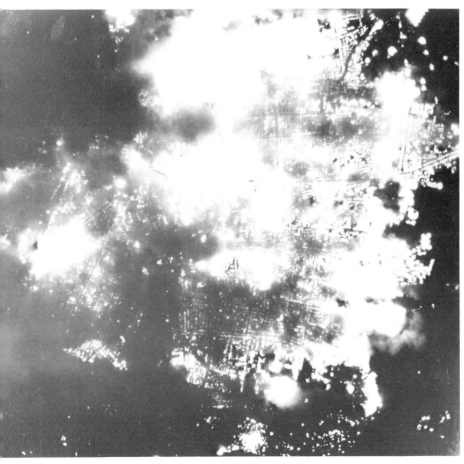

run into they didn't know what without any brakes. They were not prepared for the fact that their port main wheel tyre was burst, and as the main wheels touched down the B-24 slewed to the left out of control, its wing slicing through the tails of two parked B-25s before the two pilots could haul it back on to the runway, finally coming to rest in an area of sand. Quite an evening out! Let the USAAF historian who recorded the story finish it: 'After the two wounded gunners were sent to the hospital, the rest of the crew sat down with hot coffee to congratulate their pilot and their ship, and to contemplate the solid earth beneath them.'

It was not until the pressure of events in the Philippines reduced that serious attempts could be made to convert Japan's Formosa from an asset to a liability, but by early March 1945 things began to hot-up as the 5th Air Force started to attack airfields and the transport system. By the end of the month consistent pounding by B-24s had limited the capability of many of the enemy's air bases, and it was estimated that the approximate 600 aircraft on the island at the beginning of the attacks had been reduced by one-third.

From 1 April the island was to gain a temporary respite as the main weight of the attack was shifted in support of the forces invading Okinawa, but sufficient efforts were made in attacks on airfields that at the end of the month it was estimated that less than 100 aircraft on the island remained operational. As the demand for support at Okinawa fell off, increasing numbers of medium and heavy bombers could be deployed against Formosa.

May and June of 1945 brought hell to the island's occupants as targets were blasted by day and night. By early July it was all over: five of Formosa's main cities were virtually destroyed, its transport system useless, and industry at a standstill. Takao, the island's principal city, was little more than a pile of rubble, its harbour blocked by the wreckage of ships. Six months earlier up to 70 ocean-going ships used Formosa's ports each month: in May 1945 one vessel docked at Kiirun, and that was to be the last until the war ended in August. Vth Bomber Command, which was responsible for the major portion of these attacks, had flown 7,709 sorties, and during which 15,804 tons of bombs and 62,445 gal of napalm had been used to make a holocaust of the island. Without any need for invasion it had been rendered virtually useless to the enemy.

Meanwhile, XXIst Bomber Command had been helping in softening-up preparations for the invasion of Okinawa. In addition, as mentioned earlier, LeMay's force became involved in mining operations so that Japanese shipping would be tied up in the Inland Sea. With the pre-invasion preparations complete, the first wave of Marines – 16,000 strong – went ashore at 08.30 hours on 1 April. By nightfall this force had been swelled

WAR DEPARTMENT
OFFICE OF THE CHIEF OF STAFF
WASHINGTON 25, D.C.

25 July 1945

TO: General Carl Spaatz
      Commanding General
      United States Army Strategic Air Forces

1. The 509 Composite Group, 20th Air Force will deliver its first special bomb as soon as weather will permit visual bombing after about 3 August 1945 on one of the targets: Hiroshima, Kokura, Niigata and Nagasaki. To carry military and civilian scientific personnel from the War Department to observe and record the effects of the explosion of the bomb, additional aircraft will accompany the airplane carrying the bomb. The observing planes will stay several miles distant from the point of impact of the bomb.

2. Additional bombs will be delivered on the above targets as soon as made ready by the project staff. Further instructions will be issued concerning targets other than those listed above.

3. Dissemination of any and all information concerning the use of the weapon against Japan is reserved to the Secretary of War and the President of the United States. No communiques on the subject or releases of information will be issued by Commanders in the field without specific prior authority. Any news stories will be sent to the War Department for special clearance.

4. The foregoing directive is issued to you by direction and with the approval of the Secretary of War and of the Chief of Staff, USA. It is desired that you personally deliver one copy of this directive to General MacArthur and one copy to Admiral Nimitz for their information.

THOS. T. HANDY
General, G.S.C.
Acting Chief of Staff

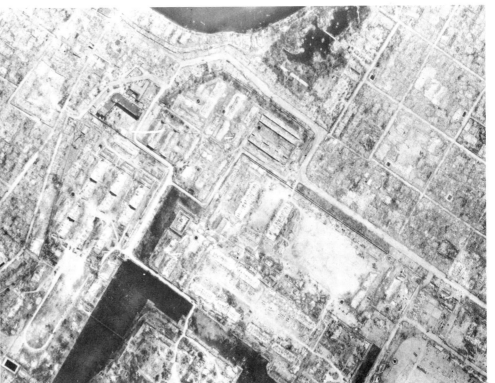

Above left: There was worse
to come. On 25 July 1945, the
top secret order for deployment
of the atomic bomb had
already been issued.

Left, above and right: Three
pictures depicting the
destruction at Hiroshima
following operational
deployment of the world's
first atomic bomb on 6 August
1945.

to 60,000 and it seemed that enemy morale might already be broken by news of the devastating attacks on the homeland, and against which there seemed little defence.

Such suppositions were premature. Although by 4 April the Marines had occupied some 90sq miles (233sq km) of Okinawa and were in possession of airfields at Kadena and Yontan, they had not reckoned on such fanatical resistance, even though Okinawa represented the last main outpost protecting the home islands.

On 6 April the Japanese launched vicious *kamikaze* attacks against American shipping and troops. And in a desperate effort the battleship *Yamato* and cruiser *Yahagi,* with a screen of eight destroyers, sailed from Toku-yama to attack the US task force off Okinawa. Despite preoccupation with the devastating *kamikaze* attacks, this fleet was spotted and vitally-needed aircraft were diverted to strike at this new threat. By the evening of 7 April the *Yamato, Yahagi* and four destroyers had been sunk. To all intents and purposes the Japanese Navy no longer existed, for this was the last action made by her surface ships for the remainder of the war.

But despite this success, the situation on Okinawa was still critical. Adm Nimitz called on LeMay for assistance and the B-29s were diverted from other tasks to strike at the airfields from which the very damaging *kikusui* attacks were being launched. Whilst reducing their intensity a little, they most certainly did not stop these activities and a total of some 1,900 *kamikaze* sorties sank at least 25 Allied vessels, as well as causing very considerable damage and casualties.

For almost a month some 75% of XXIst Bomber Command's force was employed exclusively in helping Nimitz to retain his hold on Okinawa, and it was not until 11 May that they were relieved of this task. Even then, it was not until early July that Okinawa could be considered as secure in Allied hands.

LeMay was now free to revert to his main task, the subjugation of the Japanese home islands. He was faced with two conflicting problems and it was difficult to decide which was the better method of attack. Low-level attack by night allowed the carriage of a heavier bomb load, bombing precision was not so accurate as by day, losses to enemy defences lower. The converse applied in all respects to daylight attack, but the best possible analysis showed that the pros and cons of each method just about balanced out.

Thus, it was fairly clear that for widespread destruction of an urban area the night attack was most profitable, and for precise elimination of a specific target reversion to daylight sorties was essential. This plan, in the main, was that adopted for the remainder of the war. By its end, XXIst Bomber Command had

Above left: On Saipan, USAAF crew members read details of this first horrifying attack. For them there is no realisation of the long-term implications, they understand only that, at long last, this hateful war is nearing its end.

Left: Three days later, the second weapon was dropped on Nagasaki, the characteristic mushroom cloud rising thousands of feet into the air.

Above: It, too, presented a scene of devastation to the photo-reconnaissance aircraft which overflew the remains of the city on the following day.

Centre right: Meanwhile, conventional attacks continued, and crews were briefed for new targets.

Below right: Like the pock marks of some terrible disease, bomb craters by the hundred surround the Marifu railway centre near Otaka.

dropped some 160,000 tons of bombs, including a daily average of 1,193 tons during the final three months of these operations. In so doing, they had destroyed about 40% of the built-up area of 66 cities.

It should not be thought, however, that this represented callous and unrestricted warfare against a civilian population. The productive system of Japan was very different to that of most Western countries, with a large proportion of components for both military and civil requirements being made in small home workshops. The elimination of the factories which, to a large extent were little more than assembly plants, would not have brought about widespread collapse of military production. Only by destroying the small units which provided the components for assembly could strategic attack have real meaning. And regardless of the foregoing comments there was yet another aspect of this relationship to be considered for, following formation of a Japanese People's 'Volunteer' Corps in the closing months of the war, which *made* all men from 15 to 60 years of age, and women from 17 to 40, liable

Above: On 19 August, Japanese 'Bettys' approach Ie Shima, carrying the Japanese surrender envoys.

Left: They soon acquired a mixed escort of USAAF aircraft.

Above right: On arrival, the pilots of the 'Bettys' are taken to USAAF quarters to await the return of the envoys.

Centre right: Meanwhile, the 16-man delegation is received beneath the wing of the Douglas C-54 which is to fly them to Manila for the settlement discussions.

Below right: Close-up of the delegation shows, second from left, Lt-Gen Kawabe Takashiro, Vice-Chief of the Imperial Staff, and leader of the delegation.

for defense duties, it could be argued that there were few civilians in Japan. Colonel Harry F. Cunningham of the Fifth Air Force went even further, stating in an official intelligence review on 21 July 1945 that: '. . . the entire population of Japan is a proper military target . . . there are no civilians in Japan.' This was not unfair comment having regard to the fact that he was referring directly to the above-mentioned 'Volunteer' Corps. He went on to say . . . 'We are making war and making it in the all-out fashion which saves American lives, shortens the agony which war is, and seeks to bring about an enduring peace. We intend to seek out and destroy the enemy wherever he or she is, in the greatest possible numbers, in the shortest possible time.'

There were other aspects of the task of the XXIst Bomber Command, not least of which was to destroy the productive and storage capacity of fuel oil. So important was this factor that the 315th Wing, based at Northwest Field, Guam, became delegated as the experts for dealing with such targets. Their selection had not been random, for their B-29s differed from most by having AN/APQ-7 radar equipment, which was a bombing rather than navigational system, and which enabled them to achieve pretty accurate results by day or night and in all weathers. This was precisely what was needed if Japan's limited stocks of fuel were to be eliminated as quickly as possible.

It will be recalled that the need to secure oil supplies had been the primary reason for Japan's entry into the war. This single vital commodity remained her biggest headache, for while the seizure of Indonesian productive capacity should have solved the problem, the Dutch East Indies were 3,500 dangerous sea miles (5,630km) distant from Tokyo. Her merchant shipping fleet was inadequate at the war's beginning; as it neared its end it was clear that no reliance could be placed on overseas supplies, Without the technological skill, plant and raw materials they had been unable to establish a synthetic fuel industry. The industrial and military heart was already beginning to falter from a deficiency of its essential blood stream of crude oil.

The task of the 315th Wing was to hasten up this process, a unit of vampires to suck the remaining life blood from the enemy, and a task which they carried out with considerable success. Their first strike was made on 26 June 1945, against top-priority. target, the Utsube oil refinery at Yokkaichi, and they continued to hit at similar plants or storage complexes until the war's end.

Stripped of all defensive armament, the 315th's Superforts attacked by night, often carrying a load of over 20,000lb (9,070kg) of bombs, which they dropped with commend-

Above: The long journey from Pearl Harbor to Tokyo nears its end, as Japanese surrender signatories arrive aboard the USS *Missouri* in Tokyo Bay, on 31 August 1945.

Left: Gen Yoshiro Umeza signs on behalf of the Japanese Imperial General Headquarters.

Above right: Namoro Shigomitso signs on behalf of the Emperor of Japan.

Right: For the Allies, the Supreme Allied Commander, Gen Douglas MacArthur, gives a victorious flourish to his signature. In an honoured position behind him stands, nearest to the camera, Lt-Gen Wainwright who had surrendered to the Japanese at Corregidor: behind him, Lt-Gen A.E. Percival, the British commander who had surrendered at Singapore.

able accuracy. The results were apparent to all, with oil tankers idle in the docks since there were no stocks for them to distribute.

No matter how fanatic the resistance of small groups of Japanese infantry, or the sacrifices of their *kamikaze* pilots, it was clear that the defeat of Japan was at hand. The growing success of LeMay's fire attacks left little doubt that civilian morale was falling by the day. He switched his force from the major cities and industrial targets to the secondary cities, beginning with Hamamatsu, Kagishima, Omuta and Yokkaichi on 17 June. By the end of the war the Superforts had burned out 64.85 sq miles (167.96) of the heart of some 50 lesser cities. If this is insufficiently impressive consider only Toyama, with a population of 127,860. On the night of 1/2 August 1945, all but 0.5% of its total area was reduced to ashes.

There seemed little doubt that a continuance of incendiary attacks on this scale would soon cause the enemy to sue for peace and, in fact, post war evidence confirmed the truth of this supposition. Premier Suzuki was to comment: '. . . It seemed to me unavoidable that in the long run Japan would be almost destroyed by air attack so that merely on the basis of the B-29s alone I was convinced that Japan should sue for peace.'

Thus it was clear that air power possessed the capability of avoiding the terribly costly land invasion of the Japanese islands, one that had been estimated might involve a million Allied casualties, and took no account of the total of enemy troops and civilians who would have died in the defence of their homeland.

Then, from 29 May to the end of July 1945, elements of a new unit, the 509th Composite Group, began to arrive on North Field, Tinian. They were a strange and reserved group, in the main isolated from other units on the island, and although frequently airborne in their B-29s they took no part in the general combat missions. Not surprisingly their popularity and social standing was negative.

Fortunately this attitude was not to last for long. On 6 August 1945, Col Paul W. Tibbets piloting the B-29 *Enola Gay* lifted off Tinian's runway, headed out for Japan. At 0915 hrs, 31,600 ft (9,630m) over Hiroshima, its bombardier, Maj Thomas W. Ferebee, released a new and horrifying bomb. Seconds later the world's first operational atomic bomb had shattered Japan's eighth largest city.

Statistics are inevitable to measure the effect of this single bomb. 40,653 buildings (81.1% of the city's total) were completely des-

Above: Now, at last, the mighty air armada could be turned to humanitarian rather than destructive employment. B-29s line-up on Barker runway, Saipan, to drop food clothing and medical supplies to prisoners of war.

Above right: Prisoner-of-war camps were quickly identified to facilitate air drop of supplies. This one was near Nagasaki.

Right: Now the Superforts were dropping cargoes to restore life and dignity, rather than to destroy an enemy.

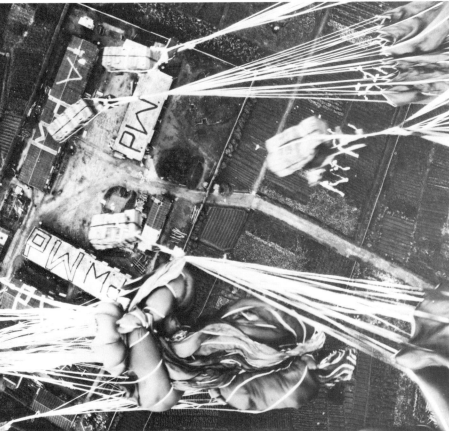

troyed, 8,396 severely damaged and 1,111 slightly damaged. More tragically, 71,379 persons were recorded as dead or missing, 68,023 injured and 171,000 homeless. When, three days later, the B-29 *Bock's Car* flown by Maj Charles W. Sweeney, dropped a second atom bomb over the port of Nagasaki, almost another 40,000 persons were killed and 60,000 injured. Japan had, indeed, reaped the whirlwind.

On 14 August the Japanese Emperor called the cabinet together and it was agreed to surrender to the US. Accordingly, a document was despatched to the Americans who, on 15 August, demanded an immediate end to hostilities. At mid-day the Emperor broadcast to his people and, to all intents and purposes, the Pacific War had ended. On 2 September, on board the battleship USS *Missouri* anchored in Tokyo Bay, Japanese envoys signed the Allied instrument of unconditional surrender. Japan's dream of conquest was at an end.

For almost four years the USAAF had fought a non-stop war against the enemy, and there can be few who will argue against the incontestable fact that air power had made an enormous contribution to victory. The B-29 campaign that had broken the spirit of the home islands would, without little doubt, have eliminated the need for physical invasion of Japan with its attendant loss of life for both attacker and defender.

It is also reasonable to assume that victory would have been achieved without the two atom bombs dropped on Hiroshima and Nagasaki. One feels compelled to ask, therefore, whether their use was necessary; if they made any significant reduction in the length of the war, or whether the destruction caused by LeMay's incendiary attacks had already spelled out the word 'defeat' to the Japanese?

Throughout a nation's history, and the no less important history of an individual, both are confronted from time to time by a signpost that points in more than one direction. Such is the nature of life that subsequently it is almost impossible to decide whether the right road was chosen. But in the case of the 'deploy' or 'not deploy' signpost of the atomic bomb, one must accept the fact that at least one physical demonstration of its awesome power was needed. It ended speedily a costly war and left little doubt in the mind of nations, small or large, that the potential horror of nuclear war which could destroy our civilisation, literally in a flash, must mean an end to all world-scale conflicts. Such awareness would never have developed from a hundred Bikini Atoll-type tests.

Ethical, moral and political decisions of this kind are not made by an air force, but by the government for which they are an intelligence, policing, punative or defensive organisation.

One orders; the other obeys. Alfred Lord Tennyson summed it up neatly, for men of all services, when he penned his immortal memoriam to the 'six hundred' of the Light Brigade:

'Their's not to make reply,
Their's not to reason why,
Their's but to do and die.'

And if you would wish to sum that up in just two words, 'patriotism' and 'courage' will do very well. They describe quite simply the motivation of the men and women of all stations, beliefs, creeds and colours that made up the United States Army Air Force, so many of whom sacrificed their lives to ensure the continuance of justice and freedom.

Above: The end of the road. A supreme moment for two men, waiting at Kadena airstrip, Okinawa, for the 'plane that will carry them to civilisation and home. They have survived three years of bestial imprisonment at Kobi: they are suffering from malnutrition and wounds: but the first dazed glimmering of salvation begins to replace the despair etched so deeply in their faces. They will serve to represent the basic elements of what we choose to call civilisation: may we learn the wisdom to preserve it.

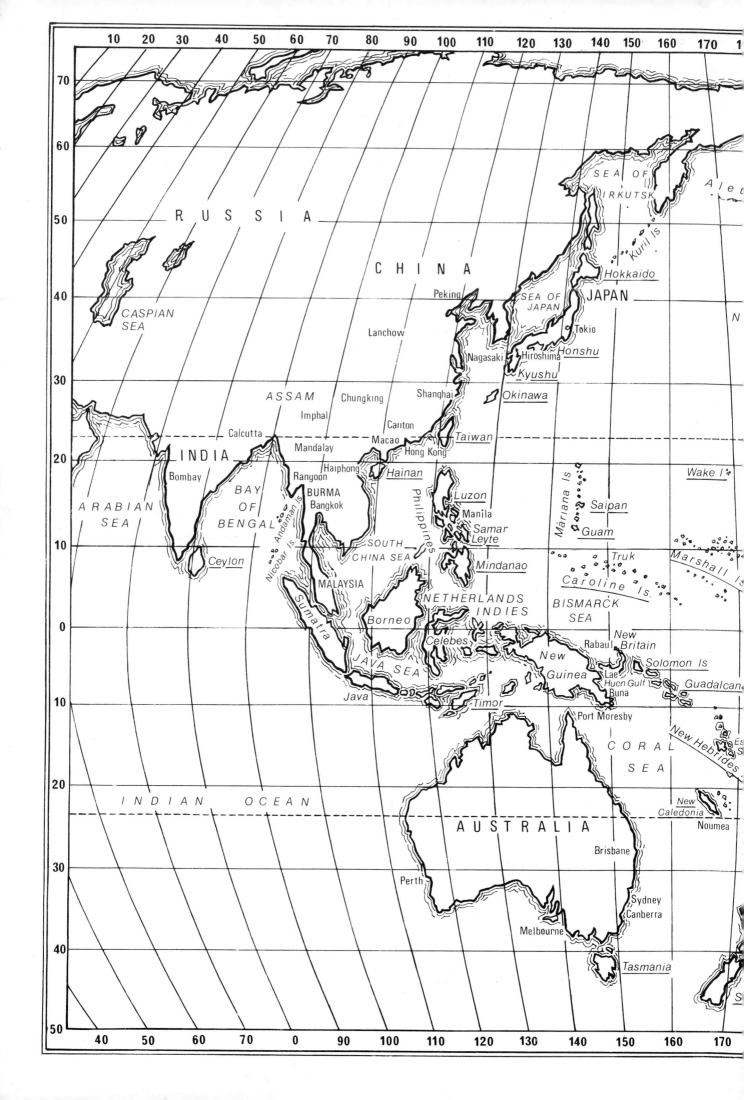